THE BABY BINDER

THE BABY BINDER

HOW "UNEXPLAINED INFERTILITY" FORCED ME TO TAKE CHARGE OF MY LIFE, HEALTH AND MEDICAL TREATMENT SO THAT I COULD LIVE BETTER AND MAKE BABIES

CALLIE MICKS

MILL CITY PRESS

Mill City Press, Inc.
2301 Lucien Way #415
Maitland, FL 32751
407.339.4217
www.millcitypress.net

Printed in the United States of America

ISBN-13: 9781545652442

DEDICATION

To the Bean and the Bear,
I would do it all again for the chance to be your mom

TABLE OF CONTENTS

Introduction

As I waited in the holding cell of a Mexican border crossing station, with fresh injection marks on my forearms, I wondered how it had come to this. Buying drugs from strangers, secret trips to Mexico, injecting myself every day. But this wasn't heroin. It was fertility treatments. And I had officially become a junkie.

Seven years later, our life is a far cry from those dark days of doctor's offices and test results and heartache. Despite the chaos of keeping up with twin toddlers - rationing out applesauce pouches and scraping stickers off the coffee table - some part of me still can't believe that we actually pulled it off. There was a time that we took incredible risks to make this happen, but I don't think we ever dared to imagine our life as parents this vividly.

We just wanted the miscarriages to stop.

I wanted to be a mom, my husband Nile wanted to be a dad. There had to be an *explanation* for my "Unexplained Infertility." A reason, and hopefully a solution. So I started knocking on doors.

Like most women, I initially put my faith and care entirely in other's hands. Repeated disappointment taught me to take control and become the general manager of my health and fertility. I learned to listen to my own instincts, to choose my own team and direct my own treatment. I also learned to loosen the death grip I had on solving this puzzle.

A fertility memoir is not merely a medical record. I thought information alone would help me solve the puzzle. But knowledge has to make friends with luck and mystery in order to bring a healthy baby into the world. The years of struggle, months of not knowing, days of utter heartbreak, they gave me more than the family I wanted. They taught me life lessons that I would not have learned otherwise.

For privacy considerations, the names in the following story have been changed. The story - and the lessons - are very much real.

PART ONE:

THE CONCEPT

CHAPTER 1

January, 2008

I realize now that motherhood does not begin when the embryo implants, or when (God willing) that precious baby gets placed on your chest. Those are some of the early experiences of motherhood, but the beginning goes back much, much further. Back to just a thought, a questioning, a trying on of the idea.

Nile and I had been married almost five years before the idea of starting a family sounded good. We'd been balls to the wall with our education and careers, and the timing never seemed quite right. At age 32, the clouds finally parted and our window of opportunity opened up. Nile completed his graduate degree, and we both landed full-time jobs ahead of the Great Recession. We didn't know what the future held, but our jobs provided enough stability for us to consider the next steps. We didn't want to get pregnant right away, but we could at least talk about it openly and start making plans.

Trying to get pregnant still felt like starting before we were ready, but it seemed like the smart thing to do. We were employed and had health insurance. Weren't those the main requirements for parenthood? I didn't want to be kicking myself later that we'd waited too long. A few years earlier, one of my coworkers had strongly cautioned me against waiting another minute to try for a baby. Kimberly was going through a difficult fertility journey herself, and as she sat across the table from me, she saw a twenty-something married girl who had the advantage of young eggs and a surplus of time. Her tales of the money and the needles and the heartache were intended to warn me, but I still wondered. *Am I really ready to become a mother? Should I let the fear of infertility push me into something I'm not ready for?*

I approach big decisions with a lot of research – the more information, the better. Plus, a little voice in the back of my mind kept telling me that this would require my attention. I was keenly aware that conceiving is not easy for everyone, but I thought I could overcome that hurdle with a little research and preparation. *That must have been what all the others failed to do.*

Thus began my deep-dive into whatever the internet could teach me about making babies. I absorbed volumes of information on the causes of infertility and took action to prevent it. When we decided to pull the trigger, I would be the healthiest, most toxin-free, absolutely fertile woman on the planet. *I can outsmart this.*

I read that you should take prenatal vitamins for 90 days before conceiving to make sure your vitamin and mineral levels were optimal. I felt like an impostor buying prenatal vitamins at Target, but it didn't stop me. Taking one pill in the morning felt like one step closer to baby every day.

I read about the threat of household toxins when trying to get pregnant. I found the Skin Deep cosmetic database* where you can type in the name of almost any health and beauty product and see it's toxicity level. I emptied out my medicine cabinet and searched each product in the database. Anything with a highly toxic rating was immediately trashed, and those with moderate ratings were cycled out at the next opportunity. Surprisingly, some of the biggest offenders were products I used every day, such as my body lotion with sunscreen from a natural foods store. Then I did the same for our cleaning supplies and other household products, researching every new thing we bought for non-toxic alternatives. Even our shower curtains were swapped out for new ones not made from vinyl or PVC, which release that toxic "new shower curtain" smell. There was no way to evaluate any immediate effects from these changes, but all of that positive change *had* to make a difference eventually. At the very least, I was creating a healthier home for the baby.

The next toxin I attacked was stress. Much of what I found online discussed the effects of stress on fertility. I've always been an anxious type of person, letting work get me all wound up. By now I knew I had to get my stress levels in check if we were considering pregnancy. Long walks or bike rides on the beach were my favorite modes of exercise, but I was still grinding and clenching my teeth at night. I needed something more to bring my stress down.

Almost everything I read about trying to conceive mentioned yoga, which had never "clicked" with me. I wasn't sure we could afford it either. A quick Yelp search directed me to a yoga studio with good reviews that was just a few blocks away from our tiny apartment by the beach in Santa Monica.

Heading there for the first time, I anticipated feeling out of place - I barely knew the basic yoga poses. But the negative thoughts pinging around in my head didn't diminish my inkling that I needed to go. The stress of my day job needed a counterweight. *Just go,* I told myself. *If you hate it, you can leave.*

The yoga studio quickly became my second home. I found myself rushing through my Tuesdays and Thursdays so that

I could hit Shannon's class at 5:30pm and then Keri Ann's class on Saturday mornings. I somehow cobbled together the money for a monthly membership; yoga seemed as essential as food, water or air. I couldn't imagine life without it.

In that studio, I met lifelong friends and teachers. I learned how to *breathe*, how to disconnect from my "monkey mind," and how to not run away when life got hard and muscles started to shake. I couldn't know then how much I would draw on these skills later. Now physically and mentally stronger from practicing yoga, I felt more "in my body" than I ever had.

There wasn't a lot of buzz back then about "self-care," but that is exactly what I was doing during this pre-conception window. I was preparing for a baby by taking care of my body and spirit more than I ever had before.

This was the beginning of my motherhood journey. Slowly peeling back the layers of myself to discover what my body needed, and what it was trying to tell me about the precarious condition of my fertility.

CHAPTER 2

August, 2008

As I was detoxing from chemicals and stress in preparation for a baby, I noticed that my menstrual cycles were not considered textbook examples of optimal fertility. I'd always known something was a little off, but I never took it seriously. All I'd previously cared about was *not* getting pregnant.

My monthly cycle was shorter than average and I had a lot of spotting. It varied from month to month, often catching me off guard and unprepared. It was strange, but I was used to it, and my doctors had always told me it was normal.

Switching my mindset from *avoiding* pregnancy to *creating* one, I started to look at my body differently.

A friend gave me her copy of *Taking Charge of Your Fertility.** I tore through it in a weekend, empowered by scientific information about female reproduction. I hid the book from Nile because I didn't want him to think I was jumping the gun. I kinda *was* jumping the gun, but it was all so interesting!

Armed with new information, I sprang into action. I tracked my menstrual cycles in an Excel chart. I bought a digital basal thermometer and put it on my nightstand to take my temperature every morning. I learned of a product called Pre-Seed, a sperm-friendly lubricant, and ordered it online. My friend Kate told me this product was the key to her two conceptions. *See? This is easy!*

The data that I collected in my charts taught me a lot about myself. From my research, both in books and online forums, I learned about something called Luteal Phase Defect (LPD). The luteal phase is the stage in a menstrual cycle between ovulation and the onset of a period. This phase can be shorted or compromised if the ovaries do not produce enough progesterone, or if the uterus doesn't respond to the progesterone. The symptoms of LPD can be miscarriages, frequent periods, infertility and spotting. I had two out of the four – frequent periods and spotting. I hadn't experienced infertility or miscarriage, but then I had never tried to get pregnant.

By charting my erratic cycles in black and white, I began to see the patterns. Based on my low temperatures and spotting during the last several days of my period, alarm bells were going off that I might have LPD.

The only way to know for sure was to ask my OBGYN to run some diagnostic tests. But, at this stage in the game, I wasn't ready to get medical help. I wanted to try naturally for a while and see what happened. I'd read anecdotes on online message boards from women who'd successfully gotten pregnant with LPD. So, it wasn't a deal breaker. Just something to be aware of.

See, we haven't even started trying to conceive and I've already found my issue. I can fix this!

DECEMBER, 2008

Nile and I were poised on the pregnancy springboard, weighing when to jump into the pool.

One morning, my phone rang. It was very early, I saw that it was my Dad calling and I answered it. His Texan accent, usually so soothing, sounded different. Pained.

"Callie," he paused for a few seconds. "I'm calling to let you know that Grandmamee died this morning." The news didn't shock me, my grandmother was 91 years old and in failing health, but anticipation does not ease the heartache of losing someone. Quietly, Dad told me about her last few hours as my love for her reoriented itself from affection to mourning.

It was my first encounter with genuine, personal loss. Before Grandmamee died, my twenties and thirties seemed like they would stretch on forever- an endless summer of freedom and selfishness. Now that she was gone, I found myself examining life through the lens of age and mortality.

Who is going to grieve me when I'm gone?

I returned from my grandmother's funeral unable to reenter life as I had left it. It felt good to come back to my own bed and daily routine, but the pattern of my life felt like a road to nowhere.

At the office, I was struck by how quickly petty things could whip my coworkers into a frenzy. Didn't they know that we are all going to die one day? And they'd wish they hadn't wasted days or years of their lives on things that didn't matter? I loved so much about my life; my well-matched marriage, my covetable job, my comfortable lifestyle just a few steps away from the Pacific Ocean. But beyond my status as a happily married, successful, beach dweller, my life lacked a deeper purpose.

Nile and I had been waiting for the timing to be right. Now it felt like "perfect timing" was not something we could man-ufacture with planning and preparation. It didn't exist at all. Time was something we could either use or lose.

My depression lifted as I processed my grief, certain now about our decision to start this new chapter. We would have liked *more* security, but we were by no means in a bad position to have a baby. Many of our friends that were in more tenuous financial situations than we were had started having kids. Somehow it all works out.

Nile and I agreed that we would "allow" pregnancy to happen, but we wanted to remain relaxed about it and enjoy our lives. We didn't feel the need to be aggressive about it. If it happened, it happened.

We were, officially, off to the races!

CHAPTER 3

February, 2009

"I'll have a cheeseburger, please, and a glass of merlot." It was Valentine's Day, and Nile and I were celebrating with a romantic dinner together. Secretly, I felt like I was celebrating a private holiday too. I had been feeling "weird." I was four days away from my period, and there had been no spotting yet. I was still new to charting my cycles, but pretty sure we had timed things really well that month.

But it was too soon to tell. I was forcing myself to wait until I had missed my period before rushing out for pregnancy tests. We were resolved to be relaxed about this, so I pushed all pregnancy suspicions to the back of my mind to avoid getting carried away. Until I had proof, it was business as usual. We clinked our glasses, and I hoped my grin didn't give me away as I lifted my wine and sipped it.

Wham! Nausea hit me immediately. As the room started to spin, I gripped the table and quickly tried to identify the most direct route outside towards fresh air or a less embarrassing place to vomit. The restrooms were upstairs, I knew I'd never make it.

Just as I spotted the closest exit, the tsunami of nausea retreated. I took a couple of deep breaths and cautiously admitted to Nile that I might possibly be pregnant; but if so, it was super, super early.

It was inconceivable to me that I would get pregnant on the first try, much less that I would be symptomatic so soon. In the back of my head, I remembered that my friend Ellenor realized she was pregnant when she'd taken a sip of a beer at a party before her period was even due and was instantly nauseous. Nile and I were skeptical. Needless to say, I did not want any more wine. I made it through dinner feeling okay, but I just wanted to go home and get in bed.

The next morning, Nile and I rode our beach cruiser bikes to our regular Saturday morning yoga class. I wasn't feeling great, and a relaxing yoga session sounded like just the thing to straighten me out.

As we settled in on our mats, the teacher set the intention for the class with some remarks about love, inspired by Valentine's Day. She talked about love and loss, and her words pierced a tender place deep inside of me. Lying there on my mat, I began to cry. As we began our standing poses, I wiped the tears away hoping they would stop. *Is this about losing Grandmamee?*

I tried to carry on. Pretty soon, we were doing vinyasas and the tears were flowing faster and faster until I struggled to breathe. I could not make it stop. But my Type-A brain refused to let me get up and leave yoga in the middle of a class. *Pull it together, girl.*

All attempts to compose myself failed. I had to get the heck out of there. I whispered to Nile that I'd meet him at home and left the room, trying to draw as little attention to myself as possible. I rode home like a mad woman, pedaling as fast as I could, blowing through stop signs while bawling hysterically. *Home. Get me home. I just want to be home.*

Finally home, I calmed down. The tears stopped and my breathing regulated. Nile had followed me back to the apartment, worried. Feeling ashamed and embarrassed, I tried to explain to him what I'd just experienced, but I still wasn't sure myself. We both knew that emotional outbursts are not like me, but neither of us knew what it meant. *Am I pregnant? Is this some new mega-PMS, or something else?*

I went to use the bathroom, and then I saw the bright red blood. Now it all made sense.

I'm not pregnant.

If I was, I'm not anymore.

Stupid me for getting my hopes up.

CHAPTER 4

The hormonal roller coaster of our crazy Valentine's Day put me on high alert. Apparently, identifying my fertile window and having sex during that time was not enough. I wanted to figure out what was going on. Had I *imagined* the pregnancy symptoms?

Many online anecdotes talked about "false pregnancy," in which women who want to be pregnant can experience pregnancy symptoms without even being pregnant. Still, I wasn't convinced that it was all in my head.

I went back to Dr. Google for answers. Based on my research, I wondered if I'd had a very early miscarriage, commonly referred to as a "chemical pregnancy." A chemical pregnancy is a miscarriage that occurs before the baby can be seen via vaginal ultrasound, usually before six weeks. I had no pregnancy test, no doctor visit, no proof at all of my pregnancy. Only my suspicions. Like a phantom miscarriage, known only to me.

I would later gain the confidence to believe my intuition without proof, but self-diagnosing my miscarriage at this point felt like a stretch. I had friends who'd had miscarriages much further along, mine felt like a little blip by comparison. It felt dishonest calling whatever I had experienced a "miscarriage."

I debated going to see my OBGYN and telling her we'd tried for only one month and got pregnant but then possibly miscarried. But I didn't want to waste time or money going into her office just to hear what I knew she would say; that 25% of pregnancies end in miscarriage and that I should just keep trying.

To be honest, I was also afraid. I didn't know what would happen once I opened myself up to the medical practice of infertility. There were too many scary questions.

Will my OBGYN even be able to help me? Can I afford it? How will I go about finding a trustworthy fertility doctor? Aren't they really expensive?

How do I even attempt this while working a stressful job? I can barely take a lunch break, how could I manage all these doctor's appointments?

I had many friends who had been down this road before me. Although I knew only a sliver of their actual experience, I knew it involved needles, pain, a lot of money and no guarantees. I wasn't ready for any of that without trying a few simple things first. If I got pregnant once by myself, I figured I could do it again. *I've got this.*

Going on the theory that I had Luteal Phase Defect because of my premenstrual spotting, I started researching online forums for natural remedies.

Many women online claimed that they had "fixed their cycle" by applying progesterone cream to certain areas of the body, like the inside of the arms, during the luteal phase. I hoped that increasing my progesterone might support a pregnancy, and avoid it ending in miscarriage.

I stopped by a local natural foods store on the way home from work and purchased the cream for about $20. Holding it my hands in the checkout line, I was excited that this little tube of cream could be the difference between baby and no baby. *See, that wasn't so hard! Problem solved!*

For several months, I applied the cream diligently during my luteal phase, even packing single-use packets when I traveled so I wouldn't miss a single application. I could tell that the cream was doing something because it had a sedating effect on me. The length of my cycle and the quality and quantity of blood flow seemed to change, but I feared it was going in the wrong direction. My cycle was getting shorter, and the spotting was sometimes heavier and darker – almost purple. It wasn't the "quick fix" I was hoping for. It didn't feel right at all. On to something new.

I tried altering my diet. I had read that going gluten-free seemed to help women conceive. Why not? It sounded like a healthy thing to do anyway. *Hey, if I lose a few pounds and get pregnant, it'll be a win-win!*

Gluten-free food was difficult for me to access at the typical lunchtime restaurants near my office, so I bought five gluten-free frozen lunches to eat at the office. I did this for a couple of days, but by mid-afternoon I was starving, raiding the candy dish or running out to get coffee for energy. For breakfast and dinner, I was just winging it; eating whatever was around as long as it was gluten-free.

I was not organized enough to handle such a major dietary switch, I felt hungry and tired all the time. Essentially, malnourished. My gluten-free diet lasted less than a week. *Why am I doing this? Because the internet says so?* I needed more than that.

Then, I read a second fertility book called Making Babies,* which helped me identify my "fertility type" and provided a week-by-week plan for a more fertile diet and lifestyle. Their program involved an overwhelming regimen of vitamins, supplements, and teas. It felt all-consuming and expensive. *How do I do all of this without becoming a crazy person?*

Looking back, I realize that that regimen closely aligns with what ended up working for me, but at the time it was too much too soon. I didn't want a significant lifestyle change, I just wanted a magic bullet – that one little thing that needed to be tinkered with to make my reproductive system fully operational.

So I moved on to maca root. My "theory of the day" was that my spotting and fertility issues were due to a hormone imbalance. Maca is an adaptogen, thought to help the body adapt to stress and boost fertility by balancing hormones. It is consumed as a powder, either added to smoothies or packed into capsules. Maca seemed a little more natural than the progesterone cream. It was worth a try.

On my lunch break, I snuck over to a mom-and-pop natural foods store and made a beeline for the supplements. A plucky employee saw me scanning the bottles on the shelf and asked, "can I help you find something?" I paused. On the one hand, I didn't want anyone to know why I was there. But on the other hand, I was there because I needed answers.

So I took a small risk and whispered, "I'm looking for maca root powder... and anything else you'd recommend to help me get pregnant." She smiled and said that yes, maca was an excellent choice and a lot of women had successfully conceived after taking it. *I knew it!*

That night, I sat at my kitchen table filling tiny clear capsules with maca powder. I experimented with different dosages at different times of my cycle, eventually adding it to a daily shot of wheatgrass that I found in the frozen food aisle at Whole Foods. The fertility plan from Making Babies included wheatgrass, so I figured, *why not nuke this by doing both at once?*

Although the maca felt more beneficial than the progesterone cream, it wasn't my magic bullet either. I began to feel uncomfortable with treating myself like a health food store guinea pig. *What if I'm making things worse?*

Progesterone cream, gluten-free food, maca, wheatgrass - I gave them all the old college try, but months ticked by and I still wasn't pregnant. Not even a little.

At the time, adding a supplement here or a cream there felt like a moderate life change. In a way, it was. I was changing my mentality, paying closer attention to my body, taking calculated steps toward better health. But "fixing" my reproductive system was going to require more than a few small tweaks. It was time to see a medical professional. If I was going to be a guinea pig, it could at least be in more capable hands than Dr. Google.

I would eventually learn to stop treating my body as a group of isolated systems and instead address it as one. One system. One objective that all systems work together to accomplish. I had to commit to making the life changes that my body needed. And, I had to be patient for the healing to happen.

But I'm getting ahead of the story.

CHAPTER 5

September, 2009

It seemed I wasn't going to find my solution at the health food store. Six months after my first suspected pregnancy, I began to sense that whatever was going on with me was bigger than wheatgrass. Convinced I wasn't going to solve the problem on my own, I made an appointment to see my OBGYN.

On the day of my appointment, I ducked out of a work meeting and raced across town to make it to Dr. Freeman's office on time. When I opened the door, every single chair in the waiting room was filled, and a couple of men (spouses, I presume) were standing. Most of the women were pregnant. The woman behind the desk stared at her computer as she asked the reason for my visit. I told her I was having a hard time getting pregnant and was here to discuss that with the doctor. She glanced up at me as if to say, *Yeah, good luck with that.*

That was my first encounter with the dismissive attitude that would define most of my fertility journey. My miscarriages were typically met with eye rolls, shrugs, a wave of the hand and a change of subject. Instead of defending my intuition, I let them convince me that it didn't matter. That it wasn't a *real* loss, or a *real* problem.

As I sat in the waiting room, an amazing number of patients filed in and out. The doctor was clearly efficient, but half an hour after my appointment time I was still sitting in the waiting room hoping it would be my turn soon. *Why did I embarrass myself at work to get here on time?*

Finally, the nurse called my name and took my weight and blood pressure on our way back to the exam room. Over an hour later, I was still lying on the elevated exam table, half-naked, scrolling on my phone to kill time until the doctor came in. *OMG, I've been here forever.*

With my phone battery completely drained, I had two choices of reading material - the baby magazines provided in the room or the hand-washing cartoon on the wall.

I don't know how long I fought off boredom and annoyance before the doctor finally came in. She was apologetic (a patient or two had gone into labor, throwing off her schedule) and asked what was going on. I told her about my experience in February. That I thought I'd gotten pregnant, but maybe miscarried. I explained to her that it seemed like something was "off" in my body, but I didn't know what. I told her about the spotting and asked if my hormones could be unbalanced.

Her response was positive and sunshine-y. She dismissed my observations and told me that I was "young, healthy and fine" and that I just needed to go home and have more sex. To be fair, she was trying to be positive. In most cases, odds were that she was right. But in my case, she wasn't. I asked if there were standard tests she could run for an initial glimpse of what was going on in my body, like for Luteal Phase Defect. She explained that half of the time the problem lies with the male partner, and handed me a business card for a lab that did sperm analysis.

When I got home, Nile and I discussed whether or not to do the sperm analysis. He was not thrilled. "Just tell me where to go and I'll do it," he huffed. He wondered how we'd already gotten to this point. Didn't we decide to be casual about this? And now we were going to a special fertility lab?

For the first time, I confessed to him that everything had changed for me back in February when I had experienced what I thought was a chemical pregnancy. My body was trying to tell me something, and I couldn't ignore it. While a sperm analysis didn't exactly address my concerns, this was the only option presented to me by the doctor. It felt like we were following breadcrumbs. *Do this test, and then the next step will reveal itself.*

The sperm analysis was our first bona fide fertility test. It's a relatively simple test, but going into a fertility clinic for the first time felt like entering a new world. It was a place neither of us really wanted to be, but I was nervously excited by the hope of finding some answers.

The good news was that Nile's lab results were very good, he was not "the problem." The downside was that we had no plan or insight from Dr. Freeman about what to do next. Our trip to the sperm lab ended with no direction, no follow-up.

So I emailed her to ask (again) if there were some basic tests that she could order to look at my hormone levels, but (again) she shrugged it off. I was at a dead end with her. I wasn't at all sure what to do next.

I proceeded with caution into this new territory. All I had was a business card for a fertility clinic and a bunch of questions.

How do I find a good fertility doctor?

Does Dr. Freeman get some sort of kick-back for referring me to one?

Will I even be able to afford it?

Do I have any insurance coverage for infertility treatments or tests?

Does this mean needles?

I was still trying to decide what my next step would be when I experienced another suspected chemical pregnancy. The same early pregnancy symptoms that ended abruptly, shoving me off the hormonal cliff. I emailed Dr. Freeman and explained what was going on. I gave a detailed list of my symptoms and attached my menstrual chart, complete with daily temperatures and other personal observations. She said that if I wanted to come in for blood work, I could. The ball was in my court. I knew the tests wouldn't reverse the early miscarriage, but they may provide some answers. That was reason enough.

CHAPTER 6

My boss was taken aback when I told her that I had a medical situation and would need to leave work in the middle of a busy afternoon. For the first time, my infertility struggle was somewhat exposed to my gossipy coworkers.

The ringleader around the office was a girl named Kirstyn. It seemed like she was always stealing the spotlight, taking credit for things she did not do, barging in on meetings where she didn't need to be and talking endlessly about how smart she was. *If you have to tell me who you are, you don't know who you are.*

Everyone else seemed to go along with it, under her spell. I was really confused. She wasn't that good at her job, and she wasn't a nice person. Why was everyone following her? I didn't understand it, so I just tried to operate outside her orbit. But it grated on me.

Now, my fertility issues became fodder for the Kirstyn-led rumor mill. *What stories will they turn this into? How many times can I get away with missing work for appointments and tests?*

When I checked in at Dr. Freeman's office, my arrival was a complete surprise to the receptionists. They did not know what blood tests needed to be run, so I sat in the waiting room while they sorted it out with the doctor. Finally, they called me into the lab room. The nurse was confused. *Which hormones was the doctor testing? What kind of answers did I expect to find?* All I did was request some basic tests for some basic answers, why were they quizzing me? Didn't the doctor know? I assumed this was routine, yet here I was explaining myself over and over again and feeling lost and foolish.

If only I had known then what I know now. That it doesn't matter how many questions you ask, there will always be more. It isn't *how much* information you gather, it's the *reason why* you're gathering it.

In the beginning, my questions weren't really a search for answers. They were open-ended outlets for my fear. Fear of not knowing what was going on in my body. Fear of what other people thought of me, what they said about me behind my back. And ultimately, fear of failure.

Fear cannot be satisfied with test results, calmed by general advice, hushed by the hints of one's intuition. I would eventually learn to let go of fear and ask questions out of curiosity. Curiosity breeds good questions, that have real answers.

Dr. Freeman called me a few days later to say that all test results were normal. I thanked her and hung up, feeling like I had just taken a detour to nowhere. To this day, I still don't know what tests she ran.

CHAPTER 7

November, 2009

As we neared the one-year mark of trying to get pregnant naturally, I watched my body for fertility cues with increasing interest. Sometimes I teetered on the line between merely observant and hyper-vigilant.

It was a fine line.

Once I learned how to identify and interpret the signs and signals my body was sending me, I started to pick up on little alerts all the time. A few months after the OBGYN appointment and sperm analysis, I started to become acutely aware of my digestive issues.

With my gluten-free experiment long passed, Nile and I shared a cookie at our local coffee shop one day. A few minutes later, I bloated up like a blimp and had sharp stomach cramps. Fertility trouble-shooting had become a part-time job by then, and celiac disease had popped up in my research as a threat to fertility. My symptoms weren't consistent with full-blown celiac disease, but my reaction to the cookie set off an alert. I resolved to talk to a doctor about it.

I was still knocking on doors, trying to find the right doctor to help me. Luckily my sweet, young primary care provider (PCP) took me seriously and ordered the test for celiac disease. I also shared my unconfirmed miscarriage experiences with her. She seemed alarmed! It came as a surprise that my just-out-of-med-school PCP was taking me more seriously than my very experienced and highly regarded OBGYN.

She referred me to a Reproductive Endocrinologist (RE) in my HMO network that she said "everyone loved." Leaving the doctor's office that day, I was practically walking on air. *Someone listened to me! Someone is testing something!*

Even though I was optimistic that the RE would have answers for me, it took a certain amount of bravery to make the first appointment with the fertility clinic. If I could put a number on it, I'd say I was 55% brave and 45% scared. The part of me that wanted to move forward prevailed this time, but fear followed closely behind, threatening to overtake my courage.

Chief among these fears was anxiety about "the shots." Some of my friends had talked about giving themselves hormone injections in airplane bathrooms and cars parked in office parking lots. That sounded like madness, almost junkie-like behavior. I'd never injected myself with anything and couldn't visualize myself doing it. *Only desperate people go to those lengths. I will be smarter than that.*

With this fear of needles as a baseline, my fear of in vitro fertilization (IVF) loomed a thousand times larger. The little I'd picked up about IVF was basically this: shots, drugs that make you crazy, vaginal ultrasound, more shots, more crazy, another vaginal ultrasound, even more shots, yet another vaginal ultrasound, last round of shots, IV stuck in arm, undergoing Propofol anaesthesia (the same drug that killed Michael Jackson), test tube babies, $12,000, no guarantee. It didn't appeal to me at all. *I am never going to do that.*

I hauled all this fear with me to the RE's office, but I was energized by the hope that he might help me have a baby. His office was in a large hospital, which lent an air of credibility and seriousness. *We are getting down to business in here!*

Looking around the waiting room, the other patients seemed to be like me. They weren't necessarily rich or crazy or old or whatever I thought fertility patients were like. I relaxed a little bit. I'd now officially moved beyond random health food store supplements and panicked emails to my OBGYN. This was the big league. *What kind of Pandora's box am I opening, and can I handle it?*

When the nurse called my name, I stood and followed her through a maze of exam rooms that led to the doctor's empty office. There was a large desk for the doctor and two chairs for the patients. I scanned the walls while I waited in silence, noting the framed diploma from an Ivy League med school and assorted photos of babies he had presumably helped bring into the world. This was all good stuff.

After a short while, a youthful, energetic and smiling Dr. Beland came into the room. Wearing a button-down shirt and tie, he appeared professional but hip. He was a doctor you'd have a beer with, just the kind of guy to help you have a baby.

After a brief back and forth getting-to-know-you conversation, he asked me how long we'd been trying to get pregnant. I explained we'd only been trying for ten months, but I had some experiences that troubled me and I thought something was wrong. He didn't seem all that concerned about my suspected chemical pregnancies, but he did say that he'd run some baseline tests that would tell us something about what was going on in my body. That was enough for me. Somebody was doing something.

Then, he launched into his spiel about other tests, procedures and fertility treatments. He rattled off a whole list of things that could be wrong and procedures and surgeries that could be in my future, including IVF. Panic set in. *Why are we talking about IVF already?*

He mentioned that he might want to do an exploratory surgery called a Laparoscopy. He explained that it was an outpatient surgery in which he would make several incisions in my lower abdomen and then insert a camera to inspect my reproductive organs. I just about fainted when he described it.

I kept a brave face through the rest of our consult, nodding my head and taking notes. But I was shaking like a leaf as I walked back to the cavernous hospital parking garage, bursting into tears the moment I was safely inside my car. I'd gone in thinking this guy was my savior, now I was picturing him slicing up my stomach like Edward Scissorhands. I wasn't ready for this. Surgeries, IVs, gurneys, recovery periods…I wasn't sure I was up for any of it.

I called Nile from the car to give him the download. He was overwhelmed too. Sitting at his desk, within earshot of coworkers, he suggested we talk at home that evening. "Don't get too far ahead of yourself," he said.

Talking to him calmed me down a little bit, and I tried to pull myself together on the drive back to work. But just as soon as my tears dried up, they would start all over again. When I arrived at work, my face was still red and blotchy from crying. I sat in my car for a little while, hoping the blotchiness would recede, but a few minutes changed nothing - I'd have to sit there for hours to totally recover. There was no way to avoid being noticed, so I walked in the door and tried to carry on with my day despite the eyes that followed me from under raised eyebrows.

That evening, Nile and I regrouped and decided to do the infertility testing and other first steps suggested by Dr. Beland. One of the tests was a Hysterosalpingogram (HSG). During this procedure, the doctor uses an injected dye and x-ray technology to determine if a woman's fallopian tubes are open. According to the online message boards I followed, it was a commonly prescribed procedure for diagnosing a cause of infertility. There were anecdotes from women claiming that they became pregnant more easily after getting their tubes flushed. *A girl can hope. Flush away!*

We arrived at the hospital and snaked our way down various hallways to the radiology department where I was supposed check-in. We found the designated waiting area, but there was no one there. We took a seat, hoping someone would come and find us. After a while, we were greeted by a young female doctor I'd never met before. She introduced herself as Dr. Beland's resident and said that she would be performing the HSG. The doctor himself would not be present. I'd never seen this woman before, and now she was going to perform a delicate and important procedure on me? Was an HSG so routine that it didn't matter who performed it? I balked. I didn't like being treated so impersonally, like cattle, but I didn't know what else to do except proceed. Besides, Nile and I had both taken the morning off of work. At this point, it felt like there was no going back.

When Nile and I separated, he turned to go back to his seat in the waiting room and stumbled over a side table. I could tell he was nervous. I was nervous too, but I understand now that it can be harder for the person in the waiting room than the one in the procedure room.

After I changed into a hospital gown, I was called into a large operating room and asked to lie on a metal table. It felt much more serious than I had expected. When I'd scheduled the appointment the week prior, the nurse told me I could take 800mg of ibuprofen "if I wanted to." I took this to mean that the procedure was minor enough that only some people needed pain relief. I had brought it with me just in case I wanted to take it afterward.

A radiologist stood nearby to make sure they got the images they needed to evaluate my uterus, tubes, and other reproductive anatomy. The resident spent about ten minutes prepping me for the procedure. A tray of cold metal instruments, a check of the monitor, an iodine swab on my cervix and we were ready. Once the catheter was in, she indicated that she was ready to push the dye into my uterus.

Next thing I knew, I was writhing on the table and screaming out in pain, trying not to move too much because moving would prolong the procedure. After a few seconds that felt like hours, she was done. The pain dulled down to a throbbing ache. *Why hadn't anyone advised me to take the ibuprofen? What else were they neglecting to mention?*

When the procedure was over and the catheter removed, I rolled off the table and shuffled back to the changing room. I felt brutalized. My insides felt raw and stretched, still throbbing. I took the ibuprofen, secured a giant hospital-issued maxi pad to my underwear to catch any leftover blood and dye, got dressed and went out to the waiting room where Nile and the drive back to work waited for me.

The good thing about an HSG is that you only have to do it once.

CHAPTER 8

Even though we were navigating the infertility world without a map, I had the support of several close friends and family members. One of my chief supporters was Marissa.

Marissa and I had been friends in college, but we'd gone our separate ways after graduation. Reunited almost a decade later when we both relocated to Los Angeles, our friendship picked up right where it had left off. We regularly met for lunch at our favorite Tex-Mex restaurant nearby, catching up and enjoying the cuisine that reminded us of home. Coincidentally, this restaurant was also the filming location of the first date scene in *Jerry Maguire*. The restaurant hung a sign over the table where Tom Cruise and Renee Zellweger sat for the movie, and we often sat there - tickled about our brush with fame. We were just two girls from Texas, after all.

Marissa and her husband were also trying for baby number one. As months became years of baby-making woes for us both, we shared many deep conversations at that table about infertility and our concerns about the future, the problems, and the odds of success.

Soon after the HSG, it was here at "our place" that she tentatively broke the news to me. She was pregnant.

She was almost halfway through her pregnancy and hadn't found the courage to tell me, but our impending lunch date coupled with her growing belly forced her hand. I imagined that she'd shared the news with some of her other girlfriends already, but it was clear that she really struggled with how and when to tell me because she didn't know how I would handle it. In fact she was crying, practically apologizing for her joyous news. I started crying too, and pretty soon we could barely eat our enchiladas.

I was so happy for her, but I was sad too because I felt more alone. She was headed down the road to mommyhood and baby showers and SUVs, and I was headed...where, exactly?

I was running out of friends who were adrift in the same "infertility" boat as me. They didn't forget me necessarily, they just had different lives. It was comforting to know that they were still there for me, but I needed more support than an occasional lunch date could provide.

My peers and I had reached that age where everyone was having babies - everyone, it seemed, except me. Even Kirstyn at work was expecting. She had told everyone in the office - except me. But I knew, of course. She sat in the cubicle next to mine, and it seemed like she called everyone she knew, fishing for congratulations and rattling on about her due date and daycare plans. She aggressively rubbed her premature baby bump like she was trying to make a genie to pop out of a bottle. I sensed she was doing it to get to me. I did my best to ignore her, but it hurt. It takes a special kind of monster to rub a woman's miscarriages in her face. *There's a special place in hell.*

CHAPTER 9

January, 2010

Two weeks after the HSG procedure, I received the official news that my tubes were clear and that all the other blood tests were fine too. We were "cleared" to start fertility treatments.

The first procedure that Dr. Beland recommended was an Intrauterine Insemination (IUI). During an IUI, the doctor injects the male partner's semen into the woman's uterus, ensuring that the sperm is in the right place at the right time to meet the egg. No drugs, no needles. The goal is just to rule out a simple mechanical problem. With my tubes freshly flushed, we were optimistic that it might make things more favorable. I liked this approach, we were still taking it slow and not rushing into fertility drugs.

Heading into our first fertility cycle, we were excited and naïve. It was almost fun - juggling ultrasound appointments, taking ovulation tests to detect the optimal date for insemination. At this stage of the game, our strategy was "divide and conquer." I did all the research and the appointment setting, and Nile made arrangements to show up if he was needed. I felt like I was dragging him along as I charged ahead, but research and analyzing is what I do well. This was what teamwork looked like, and it worked for us.

It was difficult for Nile to get away from work, so we were relieved when the ideal date for the procedure fell on a weekend. On the way to the hospital, we stopped to get a latte for him – I'd read that a little coffee before an IUI could help the sperm to swim faster to reach the egg. *What if all we need is a little caffeine?*

We sat excitedly in the waiting room – him drinking his coffee for the added "boost" and me stealing only a tiny sip to avoid upsetting the balance of my fertility. Teamwork. We felt faintly funny to be hanging out at a hospital on a Saturday morning when our friends were out brunching and drinking Bloody Marys. I had every confidence that this procedure would work. An IUI without drugs felt like all we needed.

A few minutes later, the receptionist called us to the front desk. She handed Nile the supplies to collect his "sample" and escorted him to an empty exam room. Now it was my turn to worry from the waiting room. It seemed like he was gone a long time. (He later explained that while he was trying to produce his sample, he could hear a couple of nurses right outside the door of his exam room discussing what to order for breakfast. The lack of privacy coupled with the sterility of the exam room made it very stressful and prolonged the process.)

Without sperm, there is no IUI. It's game over. There are stories of partners who can't produce on the spot, and I felt empathy for Nile and all the other men who enter that exam room under such pressure to perform. My job was easy by comparison - all I had to do was lie there.

I nervously scrolled through my phone for about forty-five minutes before Nile emerged, looking less than thrilled. He placed the sample on the counter and rejoined me in the waiting room.

I wondered how many of these we could endure. How many Saturdays and work days could we chew up sitting in a fertility clinic? We waited and waited for my turn, thinking they would call my name at any minute. As minutes turned into an hour, it felt like they'd forgotten about us. By the time they finally called us back, the excitement we'd walked in with had turned cold.

Dr. Beland came into the room where I was lying undressed on the exam table and told us that Nile's sample looked good – we had lots of happy, active swimmers. The procedure began much like a pap smear, with the insertion of a vaginal speculum. The doctor narrated each step and explained what he saw on the ultrasound machine. As he slid the catheter through my cervix and injected the sperm, Nile and I held hands. I felt a sadness that our baby wouldn't be conceived the old fashioned way, but I painted over it with thankfulness for what we had - hope.

Chapter 10

The mechanics of our first IUI cycle were pretty simple. The hardest part was all the waiting around on the day of the procedure - spending four hours at a hospital on a Saturday morning was not my idea of a good time. I was instructed to come back to the lab in two weeks for a blood draw to determine if I was pregnant. As the date for the blood draw drew closer, I caved in to the excitement and used a few home pregnancy tests. None of the tests showed a positive result, and I didn't feel pregnant. But I held out hope, because you just never know.

On the day of the test, I drove across town to have the blood drawn. Later that afternoon the doctor called and told me I wasn't pregnant. I wasn't surprised, but I was still disappointed. *Wouldn't it have been awesome if this worked?*

He suggested doing one more IUI the same way, and I agreed. We did the second procedure the following month, and all went according to plan, but that one failed as well. No chemical pregnancy, no nothing.

It was time to take things up a notch and add Clomid to the mix. Clomid is an ovulatory stimulant that increases the number of eggs released at ovulation. It seemed like a very reasonable approach. Standing in line at the CVS pharmacy during my lunch break, I was excited about this step. I'd heard so many success stories involving Clomid. Everybody has a friend or a cousin or someone they know that got pregnant on Clomid.

We started with a "natural" cycle, conceiving at home instead of at the hospital. We were ready for a break from the Orwellian hospital-conception experience.

The first few days on the drug, I noticed no reaction. But by the third or fourth day, I had a severe headache. It was so bad that I wanted to go home early from work, but I forced myself to stay, afraid of feeding the rumor mill any more than I already had. I knew Clomid was a pretty common drug, but these side effects were for the birds. A few days later, I had shooting pains in my vagina while driving home from work. I wasn't sure what that was all about, I wasn't sure Clomid was a good fit for me. *But if it works, who cares?*

Bigger concerns were looming in my mind. This was the first cycle that involved needles. I needed to do a Human Chorionic Gonadotropin (HCG) shot to trigger the release of my eggs. At the last appointment before ovulation, Dr. Beland's nurse showed me how to administer the trigger shot by grabbing a hunk of belly fat two inches away from my belly button and quickly jabbing in the needle. I felt shaky just watching her pantomime the process. *If I can't even imagine myself doing this, how will I handle the real thing?*

On the day of the injection, I drove home during my lunch break so that I didn't have to do the HCG shot in the communal bathroom at work.

Standing in my bathroom, holding the pre-filled syringe in my right hand, I simulated jabbing myself in the tummy over and over again, but each time at the last minute I'd pull it back. It felt like I was glancing off an invisible shield. The nurse had called to give me the specific time that I needed to do the shot. Every time that I chickened out, the window of opportunity closed a little more. Finally, I got annoyed enough with myself and jabbed it in. Holding my breath, I pushed the plunger to release the medicine. *I did it!*

This is how infertility is fought. Alone. With a crash course tacked on to the end of an appointment with a doctor who you wish you didn't have to see, didn't tell anyone you were seeing. Alone enough that no one hears the deep breath you take when you're facing the scariest thing you've ever done, and no one to brag to about your victories.

The pride of overcoming my fear of needles was almost euphoric. Now, I was that woman injecting herself with fertility drugs.

CHAPTER 11

May, 2010

My personal victory over the fear of self-injection gave me high hopes that this cycle would work. But it didn't. Dr. Beland recommended that we move on to stronger medications called follicle-stimulating hormones (FSH). These were injectable medications that would, ideally, produce more eggs than Clomid did. By now, I was game. Shots didn't scare me anymore, and Clomid had never felt right anyway. *Bring it on.*

The plan was to combine an intrauterine insemination with injectable FSH. I was instructed to call the office on the day that I got my period. From the moment I made that call, it was obvious that this was going to be much more involved than anything we had tried before.

On the third day of my cycle, I went into the doctor's office for a quick ultrasound. Once Dr. Beland confirmed that I was ready to go, the nurse came in to go over the drug protocol. Not only were the drugs to be injected daily (as in *every day*) but the doctor would monitor my progress via ultrasounds and adjust the doses as needed. Even the process of obtaining the drugs was more complicated. When the nurse asked me which pharmacy to send the prescription to, I replied with the address for the CVS near my apartment. She looked over her glasses at me and blinked.

The FSH drugs had to be ordered through a specialized pharmacy. It took a couple of days for me to figure out which special pharmacy my insurance used, and a few days more for them to process the order. By the time the meds arrived, it was too late for me to take the first dose on time. The office said it was no big deal, I was fine to start whenever I received the meds. I thought it was a little weird that it was okay to miss a dose, but what did I know?

Day after day, the shots got easier. The brand of FSH I was using was very user-friendly, all I had to do was place the medicine cartridge into an injection pen and dial in the dose before administering the shot. But I always double and triple checked the dosage against the protocol sheet from the doctor's office. I was afraid that messing up a dose would ruin the cycle, and all the appointments and medications and diligence would be wasted.

At the first ultrasound appointment to evaluate my eggs, Dr. Beland seemed satisfied. I didn't know yet what to expect or what questions to ask, but if he was happy, I was happy. He adjusted the drug protocol for the next few days and gave me instructions on when to do the trigger shot to release the eggs. I wouldn't see him again until the IUI.

By now the process was fairly familiar to us, and there was some comfort in familiarity. I still had romantic notions of conception and wanted Nile to be in the room when we "conceived" our baby.

He sat in a little chair in the corner near my head as I laid naked from the waist down on the table, just like the previous two IUI's. But this time, Dr. Beland came in accompanied by three unexpected guests. Two of them were fresh interns, and the third was the resident that had flushed my tubes. As they entered, Nile stood up from his chair because, with six adults crammed into a tiny exam room, it was now standing room only.

They each introduced themselves and extended their hands to shake mine. Not knowing what else to do, I propped myself up on my left elbow and reached my right hand across my body to meet theirs. Shake, nod, *nice to meet you*, smile. Shake, nod, *nice to meet you*, smile. Shake, nod, *yes, I remember you*, smile. Nothing like a meet and greet while lying half naked on a table, feet in stirrups, a flimsy piece of paper draped over my lower half.

Dr. Beland sensed the awkwardness of the situation and tried to adjust the set-up of the room to accommodate everyone plus the equipment. They were each very respectful of me and were trying to stay near my head even though there was more standing room by my feet. I appreciated his efforts but would have preferred not to have all these people in the room. This process still felt sacred to me. Sure, it's clinical too, and this is a teaching hospital, but again, I felt like cattle. Cattle that were being studied in a lab experiment having to do with their sex organs.

Luckily, the IUI procedure itself went pretty smoothly. It took longer this time because the doctor carefully explained each step to the interns. But it was over soon enough. It wasn't the best experience, but if this cycle was the one that worked then it wouldn't matter.

I truly was more hopeful this time because we had used stronger drugs. Again, the doctor wanted me to do a blood test to confirm the pregnancy about two weeks after the IUI. I counted down the days like I was a kid waiting for Christmas. The first week was the hardest, but as I got closer and closer to the day of the pregnancy blood test - commonly referred to as a "beta" - the wait became easier.

I didn't have any pregnancy symptoms to speak of, but I knew that some women have no symptoms. I did my best not to obsess about whether it had worked or not, but that was impossible.

I dragged Nile to the lab for the blood test, which fell on a weekend. I wanted him to share the whole experience, not just the part that required his contribution. Once they had my blood sample, we left the lab and went on with our day, waiting for the phone to ring.

Finally, mid-afternoon, Dr. Beland called. He apologized for calling us while driving in the car with his family present. Again, I felt as though more strangers had been invited into my metaphorical bedroom as he informed me over speakerphone that I was not pregnant.

CHAPTER 12

It had to be hard for Dr. Beland to make those phone calls day after day, informing his patients of the news (most often, the bad news.) He tried to sound cool and upbeat when he called us from his car to say that the last round of interventions had failed.

I was crushed. We'd been methodically escalating the amount of intervention, and it still wasn't enough. This "getting pregnant" business was harder than I had imagined. Dr. Beland suggested we repeat the same protocol right away – an IUI with injectable FSH. *Ok, let's do this.*

Fertility treatments are often compared to gambling in Las Vegas. Most people pay out of pocket for IUI and IVF, procedures that statistically aren't likely to work the first time. Signing up for one of these procedures is akin to putting a lot of chips on the table, knowing they will likely be swiped away and taken to the vault. But you keep scraping together more chips, hoping one day you'll beat the odds and hit the jackpot - which in this case is a baby. However, our most recent IUI failure gave me a deeper understanding of the Vegas Fertility analogy.

For six months, we had gradually increased our infertility treatment game. First with two IUIs with no drugs, then a Clomid cycle to get my body to make more than one egg, and finally an IUI with injectable meds, which is about as far as you can take an IUI.

But none of them had worked. As we stair-stepped our way up through these interventions, I became less risk-averse; shirking my fear of needles, hoping I was getting closer to the finish line. Even the failed cycles made me feel like I was acquiring new skills and new knowledge and, in some small way, made me feel like a winner. I was still in the game, and the only way to win is to stay in the game. It felt good to bounce back and immediately try again. We were doubling down. The more cycles we did, the more we increased our odds.

The unexpected side-effect of this try-try-again attitude was that we weren't allowing ourselves to process what was really happening. The optimism of the doctor, the statistics of success, the students in training - all of it focused on our fertility as a medical puzzle to be solved. There was no time or emotional energy for disappointment, or even loss.

Every interaction with my doctor ended with a plan for moving forward, but never a plan for healing from what had already happened. There was no talk of seeing a counselor about the suspected miscarriages, or how the emotional and financial stress may have been affecting our marriage. It was all scientific.

When you get sucked into the science of infertility, it's easy to forget that that's not all there is. There is loss, there is love, there is intuition and a hundred other unquantifiable forces at play. The doctors are there to guide you through the medical stuff, but you also need to find your own guides to help you navigate the rest of it.

By relying solely on my doctor, I failed to treat the whole problem because I failed to recognize all of its parts.

CHAPTER 13

July, 2010

After the disappointment of our third IUI failure, I
wanted to get back on the horse because it gave me
something to look forward to. It seemed rational to repeat
the IUI cycle with injectable FSH meds before moving on to
something else.

The second cycle went much like the first one, with the same
special-order drug protocol and ultrasound monitoring. I
injected as instructed, but when I arrived for my first ultrasound to check on the progress, the resident explained that
my egg follicles were growing too fast, with the lead follicle
already reaching a mature status. My right ovary, where the
large follicle was, felt like an overfilled water balloon ready
to burst.

They wanted to do the IUI a couple of days later, on the tenth
day of my cycle. That didn't seem right to me, it seemed

much too soon. In all my internet research, I had never heard of IUIs being performed this early. Not successfully. Plus, the resident's tone was kind of panicky. Something seemed off.

With the IUI date set for a few days earlier than anticipated, there wasn't enough time to order the trigger shot through the pharmacy. The resident rifled through what seemed like every drawer in the office and found one for me, a sample from the pharmaceutical rep.

I didn't feel good about this cycle at all, but I also did not have the nerve to ask questions or tell the doctor "no." I was along for the ride. Besides, there was no putting the genie back in the bottle now. These follicles were going to ovulate no matter what I did.

Since I had very low hopes for this cycle, I let Nile sit it out. He produced his sample at home, and I drove with it between my legs to keep it close to body temperature. Yet another doctor I'd never met came into the exam room to perform the IUI. Not surprisingly, that cycle didn't work either.

I couldn't believe that all five cycles had failed, without even a chemical pregnancy. We were now a year and a half into this journey and felt further than ever from the finish line.

I wasn't sure what to do next, but I felt that it was time to fold my cards and regroup.

When I was ready, I scheduled a follow-up appointment with Dr. Beland. Some people refer to it as the "WTF appointment." I wanted to know What The F**K had gone wrong with the five cycles, and I hoped the doctor could give me some insight into what was happening and what steps we might take next.

Dr. Beland didn't have any concrete answers or plans based on my history, instead giving me an off-the-cuff explanation and generic "go forward" strategy. He glanced very briefly at the pages and pages of information included in my chart and basically shrugged his shoulders and said I should do in vitro fertilization. He rattled off something about the lab where they make the embryos and that the nurse would give me all the information about the costs, et cetera. It didn't feel right to me.

I was 33 years old with a diagnosis of Unexplained Infertility (which is no diagnosis at all) and a history of getting pregnant without any help at all, and a partner with a good sperm analysis. Nothing – not my medical history, not the doctors – had convinced me that IVF was the answer.

I told him I'd think it over, which I did. I wasn't ready to take on the escalating cost and risk of finding a private fertility doctor. On the other hand, staying with this doctor meant IVF, and that was even scarier. I didn't have the knowledge or experience to say what I thought my treatment should be, but I had a feeling that pursuing IVF now, with him, was a bad idea.

My intuition was kicking in. My instincts were telling me that I wasn't in the right hands, and I decided to walk away.

CHAPTER 14

M oving on from my first fertility doctor, I now had big decisions to make regarding our next steps. *Okay, Google. Do I seek high-tech medical intervention or find a holistic approach? Are there other paths forward that don't involve IVF?*

I was daunted by the cost of fancy fertility doctors and the volume of injections. On the flip side, doing nothing didn't feel right either. And, I'd already ruled out wheatgrass.

I knew I needed to do *something*, but I had more questions than answers. I had a couple of friends who I could go to for guidance, but I worried that I was leaning too heavily on them, unfairly treating them as a therapist. As grateful as I was to have friends that would hear me out, I didn't want my infertility to be the only thing we talked about, nor did I want to be a needy friend, looking for help in the wrong places, sucking blood from a turnip.

It's the catch-22 of infertility support. Even when you have a friend who understands, depending on them to meet your huge demands for emotional support could kill your friendship, and then you'd have no one. Either way, it's lonely.

I'd heard of an organization called Resolve that hosts online and in-person infertility support groups. Naively, I had hoped that my infertility would not progress to the point of needing a support group. I'd been pretty active on the infertility message boards on Babycenter.com, but with two years of intervention and no baby, I felt like I'd graduated from that community. The few "friends" I had made in online fertility forums vanished as soon as they got pregnant.

I realized I needed something more - something real - so I looked up Resolve.org. There, I found an extremely well-organized website with loads of information and support. I spent several weeks thinking I could thrive on the resources they provided on their website and participating in the online message board. But eventually, I had to address the emptiness that had brought me there in the first place – my need for better, more tangible support. So, I plugged my zip code into the "Find a Support Group" search box.

I worried that my work schedule and the insane LA traffic would make it logistically unrealistic to attend a group meeting. I couldn't afford a therapist in addition to fertility treatments, so I crossed my fingers and hoped for the best. As soon as the search results came up, I discovered there were two different support groups near me.

This was the moment of truth. *Do I hide behind the glow of my computer screen, connecting with women anonymously, or do I do the scary thing and reach out and make myself seen?*

I talked myself into at least emailing the contact person listed for the group that was closest to my office and held meetings on weekday evenings. If they responded, I still wasn't obligated to do anything with the information they provided.

The organizer replied to me almost immediately with a welcome message. She explained that she was no longer hosting the group herself (I later learned it was because she was pregnant), but she provided all the information about the next meeting. The ball was in my court.

The next meeting was only a few days away. I mulled over whether or not to go. I felt scared, vulnerable. I'd never been to a support group before, and I wasn't sure what to expect. My idea of a support group was akin to the famous "you had me at hello" scene from Jerry MacGuire. *Is it going to be a bunch of desperate women sitting around crying and bitching about how horrible their lives are?*

I wasn't sure whether being in a room with dozens of infertile women would make me feel weighted down or lifted up, but there was only one way to find out. It felt like I was still one foot in and one foot out of the fertility community. I resolved to try it with the same caveat that I used the first time I tried yoga. *If it's not for me, I can leave.*

CHAPTER 15

As a Texan living in California, I often felt like a potted plant that had been shaken out of a cramped but cozy pot and replanted into a new one that was too large. California certainly agreed with me, but there were pros and cons to being a small fish in a large pond. Even though I'd been in LA for almost four years, I was still learning how to find my way around this sprawling city. Chatting with my mom on the phone, I lied and told her I was on my way to happy hour with some work friends.

As I drove south along the Pacific Ocean from my office to the Resolve meeting, the setting sun painted the sky spectacular strokes of orange, pink and purple. Although I was nervous and a bit keyed up about the meeting, I was comforted by that familiar sky, driving down a familiar road toward a decidedly unfamiliar destination. Part of me wished I was driving the other direction, toward home, where everything was safe and predictable and unchallenging. But I wasn't. I was driving toward discomfort and a room full of crying women.

Snaking my way inland a bit, I realized I was in my friend Marissa's neighborhood. She had just welcomed her baby boy into the world the previous week. I was so excited to meet him that I played hooky from work to be one of their first visitors in the hospital. I was relieved to realize that I could be happy for her and sad for me at the same time.

Driving past our lunch haunt on my way to the Resolve meeting reminded me that the pond wasn't so big after all. I took it as a sign that I was headed in the right direction.

Eventually, I pulled up and parked outside a modest home in a quiet tree-lined neighborhood in West LA. I sat in my car for a few minutes and watched as two other women walked to the front door of the hostess's house. They *looked* normal. Denying my anxiety, I summoned the courage to get out of my car, walk up to the door, and ring the bell. The hostess answered the door and welcomed me warmly. Walking me into the living room, she offered me a drink and gave me a quick rundown of the set-up and structure of the meeting.

The meetings were held twice a month at the home of a member of the group. Occasionally, meetings were also held in a conference room in an office or residential high-rise building, depending on who was hosting. Chairs, sofas and other available furniture were arranged in a circle in the living room to accommodate as many women as possible. Attendees brought snacks and drinks to share – sometimes including wine. The group wasn't exclusively for women, but I soon learned that men rarely, if ever, attended.

There was no requirement to share anything at all. Generally, each woman would share a concise version of her story, where she was in her infertility journey, and ask any questions she had for the group. We went around the circle until everyone who wanted to had spoken. In fact, this scene was pretty similar to the one in Jerry MacGuire. Except this was real. I was standing on sacred ground. The heartbreak, the worry, the tears… this was real life, and no heartthrob was coming to save us.

At first, I didn't have that much to share. My story was short. It was basically, "I think something is wrong with me, but I don't know what." Many of these women gave me that same look that my OBGYN had - that I was young, healthy and fine and that I should just go home and have more sex. Some of these women were a decade older than me and had been down a long, tough road. A road I would eventually go down, too.

I continued going to the meetings month after month, soaking up everything. Over time, I felt more comfortable asking for the support and advice I needed. As I gained experience, I even felt confident chiming in and giving advice or comfort. I felt safe with this group. What I learned from these women was absolutely a springboard for my own journey and eventual success.

At that first meeting, I didn't know how much I would grow to depend on my Resolve group for support. I thought we were near the end, that the next intervention would work or my body would magically begin to make healthy babies. As it turned out, on our road to having kids, we had barely left the driveway.

PART TWO:

EVERYTHING BUT THE KITCHEN SINK

CHAPTER 16

Nile and I continued to try for a baby naturally, hoping we'd get lucky and avoid the fancy fertility doctor step altogether. But that wasn't meant to be. Six months had gone by since we'd parted ways with our fertility clinic and we weren't pregnant. Not even a whiff. It was time to move on.

The women at my Resolve support group provided the names of the "good" fertility doctors in the area. Living in Los Angeles, we were very fortunate to have several highly regarded clinics to choose from not too far from our house. Two names kept coming up over and over again amongst the rotating attendees of the support group, Dr. Gilpatrick and Dr. Silberman. These two REs shared the same practice, and their clinic was only ten minutes from my house. My last RE was located inside a hospital that was more like thirty minutes from my house, plus $15 for parking each time. A clinic that I could easily pop into on the way to work was critical, with all these obnoxious appointments *plus* a demanding job. So choosing my new clinic was easy, now I just needed to decide which doctor.

I still struggled somewhat with the notion of going to a private fertility clinic. Even though I felt as if I had been just a number with my last RE, I liked the democracy of a hospital; the doors were open to everyone.

Switching to a private fertility clinic, I wondered if I'd be treated as well as their celebrity patients. I'd heard rumors of a private waiting room for celebrities, separate from the civilian one that we used, but I never saw it. I once saw a well-known actress make a clandestine exit through a back door of the parking garage and into the alley where a hired car was waiting for her. One of my friends at the Resolve support group told me she had once ridden in the elevator with an A-list singer who was married to an A-list actress. He was wearing a ball cap and looking down, but it was obvious to my friend who he was. Separate waiting room or not, apparently nobody escapes that elevator.

As I read the bio for each fertility doctor on the clinic website, I felt like I was playing "Eeny Meenie Miny Mo." They were both highly qualified, and highly rated. In the end, I went with the RE who was originally from my home state. I called it fate. This man *had* to be the one who could solve my problem, because he was a Texan.

Even in LA, with lots of doctors to choose from, it can take a while to get a consult. We got lucky. January is a slow month, so we only had to wait a couple of weeks for our initial consultation appointment.

I spent those two weeks trying to gather my records – test results, charts, x-rays, blood work. The amount of paperwork was ridiculous, and hounding the various departments to fill my requests became a demanding and tedious task.

Most of the records were sent straight to the new fertility clinic, but all that hunting and gathering made me realize that I needed to start requesting copies of all my test results from then on for my own records.

This called for a binder. I considered swiping one of the discarded binders from my office, but I didn't like the juju of that idea. Anything coming into contact with me and my fertility journey should have positive energy. Scanning the shelves at my local office supply store, my eyes rested on a bright pink binder. For something as drab as medical records, a pop of color felt right. *When in doubt, choose happy.*

By now, I had learned that infertility is a lonely journey. Even when you find doctors and friends that support you, their presence is almost always temporary. It was clear to me that I needed to take more control of my situation. I needed to keep my own center of gravity so that I didn't lose balance every time a piece of my support system disappeared.

Chapter 17

January, 2011

Our consultation finally rolled around, and I was barely recovered from a case of the flu that had side-lined me for days. Feeling human again, I was excited to be moving forward.

Nile met me at the clinic, our cars swooping into the parking lot at the same time. We walked to the front door hand in hand, approaching together this brave new world.

We scrolled through the electronic directory to get buzzed in. The sound of the traffic on the street was so loud that I put my ear right next to the speaker to hear the person on the other end. Person on the other end says something that I can't make out, and I say, "We're here for our consult with Dr. Silberman." *Buzz, buzz, buzzzzzzz.*

We rode the elevator from the lobby to the top floor, where we entered a beautifully appointed, professional, soothing and light-filled space. Turning to our left, we approached the reception desk - a custom work of art itself, incorporating fertility symbols and natural materials into the design. *It's fertility Mecca up in here.*

We checked in, the receptionist said that the doctor would be ready for us very soon. The waiting room was pretty empty since, I assume, most of the action happened in the morning as it had at our last clinic. As we sat down, Nile turned to his phone for distraction, but I looked around to take everything in. They must have spent a *fortune* on the interior design alone. A few women came and went (patients I assumed) and I tried to size them up. *Are they normal? Are they bazillion-aires? Are they famous? Do they look desperate?*

After a brief wait, we were escorted into Dr. Silberman's sunny office where he was waiting for us. As soon as he opened his mouth to greet us, I was instantly put at ease. He had a warm, relaxed presence. Despite his decades in California, he still had a Texan accent as strong as the day he left. Just listening to his drawling small talk made me feel right at home. *This is the man that will fix me.*

CHAPTER 18

I t was exciting to make plans for moving forward with a doctor who addressed all of my concerns - even the ones I had kept to myself. Dr. Silberman came across as smart, methodical, experienced, confident, warm... all the things my previous doctor wasn't. It was like night and day.

Dr. Silberman believed that the IUIs we had done before basically needed to be thrown out. He never said a disparaging word about my prior RE, but explained why the protocol used before didn't meet his standards. He also said our last IUI should never have been carried out because the drugs from the previous cycle had altered my hormones to the extent that adding more at the start of the next cycle was not going to result in mature, viable eggs.

From the outset, his assessment confirmed what I had intuitively believed all along. It struck me just how clear, confident and matter-of-fact he was. *Maybe I wasn't crazy. Maybe I was right!*

He wanted to run a couple of blood tests first, but he felt confident that we were ready for an IUI with injectable FSH using a better protocol. I left the meeting with everything I wanted from a doctor's appointment - clear action steps and confidence that I was in good hands.

One other thing proved to me that Dr. Silberman was right for me - he suggested adding holistic treatment to the mix. He recommended a Chinese medicine doctor, Dr. Zheng, and suggested that I begin receiving regular acupuncture treatment.

Dr. Zheng was a well-known acupuncturist in my infertility circle, I was sure that she had treated some of my peers. I might have sought her out sooner, but I doubted that we could afford the $100 weekly visits for months and months on end. I didn't want to start something I couldn't finish. My faith in Dr. Silberman was just the push I needed.

At our first appointment, Dr. Zheng did a full intake of my medical history. Being familiar with Western medicine, she wanted to know about the tests and procedures I'd been through and their results.

Then, she did something that no one else had bothered to do. She asked about my miscarriages.

Up until that point, those early pregnancies had only existed in my mind because no doctor had ever confirmed them. I told her about the symptoms, the sudden emotional outbursts. As I recounted them to her, I found myself doubting their reality. *My pregnancies were always over before I even knew they had begun, what if I was making it all up?*

Instead of brushing it off as irrelevant, she took my experiences very seriously. She gave me permission to believe that it was real, despite there being no medical proof. And permission to grieve my private loss.

After a physical examination, Dr. Zheng laid out some diet guidelines and asked that I chart my body temperature each morning for her to review. She prescribed a daily cup of tea, made from Chinese herbs that she would blend for me after every visit.

She asked me to pause all fertility treatments for six months. I nodded my head to show that I understood her request, but I knew I didn't have it in me to comply. I was already three years into this process, and I had my amazing new Texan doctor who was ready to get started. I couldn't sit it out for another half year.

At the risk of offending my new acupuncturist, I decided to do both - to move forward with an IUI with Dr. Silberman *while* getting acupuncture. I still had doubts about how much acupuncture could really help, finding mixed results from academic studies on the subject. At the very least, it was proven to increase blood flow in the uterus,* which couldn't hurt.

A few days after my initial appointment with Dr. Zheng, I got my period and called the fertility clinic to get the ball rolling.

CHAPTER 19

Our first IUI with Dr. Silberman was easy. The nurses were much more helpful and available to answer questions than we'd found at the prior clinic. The doctor was always on time, reducing our overall time commitment considerably. The exam rooms were more spacious and soothing. Even the sperm collection room was a big upgrade from the hospital clinic, with comfy furniture and a shockingly diverse selection of porn. This clinic was a well-oiled machine.

Everything about this cycle seemed great! My egg follicles were doing what Dr. Silberman wanted them to do, and the IUI went off without a hitch. I went home to rest and tried not to obsess about the outcome. About a week after the IUI, I started noticing what I thought were pregnancy symptoms. Each one of my suspected pregnancies had had different symptoms, but they all pointed to the same thing. It always felt like something was taking over my body, like a light switch inside of me had been turned on. Now, I was feeling that same shift.

I started taking home pregnancy tests each morning. The first test I took was positive. Faint, but positive. I didn't allow myself to get excited because the "trigger booster" shot prior to the IUI can cause pregnancy tests to give a false positive. Time would tell. I continued to test at home, and the tests were still positive, but still faint. I noticed symptoms on and off, but my work kept me just distracted enough not to fixate on my hopes.

At my weekly acupuncture session with Dr. Zheng, she was very positive about this cycle and told me that she thought I was pregnant. This wasn't a wild guess (she knew the consequences of getting my hopes up) she was *sure*. The skeptic in me questioned whether she could really detect a pregnancy from my pulse, but the rest of me wanted to believe that it was true. *One IUI with my hero doctor and we're pregnant!*

I was walking on air. I just had to wait until after the weekend so the pregnancy could be confirmed via blood test on Monday.

But the day after Dr. Zheng's premonition, everything stopped. Just like before. My hormones went off a cliff and my uterus felt heavy, like my period was coming. Looking at the positive pee sticks lined up on my bathroom counter, I tried to remain hopeful, as if staring at them hard enough would reverse whatever was happening.

I was scheduled to get a pregnancy blood test the next day if I hadn't gotten my period. If I could just make it one more day without bleeding, then I could still cling to the hope that all was not lost.

As I was preparing to leave for the clinic on Monday morning, my period hit. I had sensed it was coming, but was disappointed that my first real "beta" had just been snatched out of my hands.

I called the clinic anyway and scheduled an appointment to discuss the past cycle and perhaps start another one. Dr. Silberman was out that day, and Dr. Rollins would be subbing for him. I'd seen Dr. Rollins around the office and wondered about her. I hadn't heard much about her in the Resolve meetings, but she had great energy and plenty of patients.

She entered the room with a smile on her face and quickly got down to business. She performed an ultrasound to see if I was able to cycle again and discovered a cyst in one of my ovaries. This made sense to me because I had some throbbing pain on that side. She said the cyst should go away on its own, but we'd have to sit that cycle out.

When I went back in for my weekly appointment with Dr. Zheng, she was shocked. She had been so confident, saying she "knew" I was pregnant. I thought I knew it too. She gave me special herbs and needle placements to help get rid of the cyst.

One of the things Dr. Zheng had asked during our initial session was if I had been tested for autoimmune issues, like antiphospholipid antibodies (APA) or natural killer (NK) cells.

At the time, I was so gung-ho to start working with superstar Dr. Silberman that I didn't want to delay our first cycle. I'd heard about an autoimmune component to recurrent miscarriage, but I hadn't yet explored it for myself. When she brought it up again, it seemed worth considering.

Even though we were with a new clinic, it still felt like I was paying people to prove what I already knew - I could get pregnant, but I was miscarrying. We needed to stop focusing on how to *get* me pregnant and figure out how to *keep* me pregnant.

Eventually, I decided that I wanted to do the tests that Dr. Zheng recommended. A few women in my Resolve support group had had the tests done, but it was awkward for me to call up the famous fertility doctor and ask him about these tests. From his point of view, we had only done one legitimate IUI cycle. It's not typical to run a full miscarriage panel after one failed IUI (which resulted in an unconfirmed chemical pregnancy). *Wouldn't he have ordered them if it was relevant to my case?*

On the other hand, I knew I was miscarrying, and Dr. Zheng felt that these tests might give us answers. I needed answers. I knew my body more than anyone, and now Dr. Zheng had mentioned these tests twice. I didn't want to waste $200 on an office visit, so I called Dr. Silberman's nurse and asked about having these tests run. The nurse called me back after discussing it with the doctor and said that it was basically up to me if I wanted them to order the tests. I said yes.

I went to the lab at the clinic to have my blood drawn for the tests. As the lab tech filled five vials with my blood and prepared them for shipment to the special testing lab in Chicago, I sensed that something had shifted: I was starting to direct my own care.

Requesting those tests marked a pivotal point in my health-care journey. Before, I would present my case to the doctor and submit to their final judgment. Even if it didn't make sense to me, even if it went against my intuition, I trusted their verdict above all else because they were, after all, experts in medicine.

Now, I realized that it didn't take an expert in medicine to put the puzzle together. It took an expert in *me*, Callie, and I was the foremost authority on that subject. My doctors were like valuable team members, and I would continue to approach them with the respect that they deserved. But this was *my* team. I decided who was in, and who was out. From this point on, I was ultimately responsible for solving my infertility and determining my treatment.

About a week later, I got a call that the results of the APA and NK tests were normal, which seemed to rule out auto-immune issues as a factor. Normal was good of course, but I felt no closer to finding out what was happening in my body. Unsure which theory to explore next, I felt the only way forward was to do another cycle.

We did a second IUI with Dr. Silberman four months later, our sixth one overall. It was a picture-perfect cycle, just like the previous one. We had every reason to be hopeful, but it didn't work. Not even a hint of pregnancy. The odds of success were less than 20% anyway. Still, it was a bummer. It left us at a complete dead end. And, at $2,000 a pop for each IUI cycle, our bills were adding up.

CHAPTER 20

I felt defeated after the "fertility doctor to the stars" couldn't get us pregnant either. We hadn't even moved on to IVF yet, but I didn't like that LA's best RE didn't know why the IUIs didn't work, or why the first one worked but I didn't stay pregnant. If embryos had implanted in my uterus before, how would IVF improve anything?

I didn't know which direction to take next. I'd researched several diagnostic and exploratory procedures that we hadn't considered yet, such as a laparoscopy, and compiled a list of possible things to try. But the infertility roller coaster had completely exhausted me, and I decided to get off.

I wanted to try naturally for a little while, going the holistic route once again. Perhaps I should have listened to Dr. Zheng and dedicated the full six months to her acupuncture and Chinese herb protocol only. *After all, I don't need to pay a fertility doctor thousands of dollars for something I can do for free: miscarry.*

One thing that had been nagging at me was my work environment. I dreaded going into work. A creeping anxiety would come over me every Sunday night and gnaw at me on my drive to work each morning. I clenched my jaw so tight at night that I always woke up with teeth marks on my tongue. The actual job was pretty good, but the environment was toxic. And with the cost of living in coastal California, unemployment was not an option. I didn't have the luxury of disliking my pretty-good job.

I kept telling myself that there was no reason for me to be this stressed. But all the positive thoughts, yoga, aromatherapy and deep breathing in the world wasn't enough. My body was screaming at me, telling me I wasn't on the right path.

I needed a change. I didn't know whether I just needed a different employer or an entirely different career. I didn't know if it would require going back to school, or taking up hobbies in search of my "passion," or if the expense of the fertility treatments would eventually send me crawling back to the same poisonous office. All I knew was that it wasn't physically or mentally healthy to put myself in the situation I was in every day.

I found guidance in the advice of renowned life coach Martha Beck. She taught me to follow my animal instincts. That a "good job" on paper can still make you miserable if it's the wrong job for you, and the only solution to that problem is to move on to something else. She also writes that when you have to choose between several options, choose the path that feels like freedom. The thought of staying in my current job made my whole body tighten and my jaw clench; freedom felt like not having to go there anymore.

Nile and I agreed that I could quit my job. We knew that I'd have to return to the workforce eventually, but the moment we made that decision I instantly felt free.

Standing in my boss's office, I explained that I needed to leave the job to focus on my health, but felt I could still manage our biggest client from home. After some negotiations with HR, we agreed that I would continue working as an independent contractor - I was free to keep my job and work from home!

We decided to tell the team at the next staff meeting. At the end of our routine business agenda, my boss prompted me to announce that I was leaving the company. There were a few girls who looked genuinely heartbroken about me leaving, which was bittersweet for me. I was glad that our friendship ran deeper than just office cordiality, as I'd hoped it did. But sad too, to be leaving a few true friends behind.

Suddenly, from her end of the table, Kirstyn announced that she had something to say. "I'm pregnant!" she shrieked. I wanted to yell, *"We know!"* She had already told everyone in the room – everyone but me. But my announcement had, briefly, taken her spotlight away, and she was scrambling to steal it back from her unwilling rival. All hail the queen -- off with my head! If I had had any doubts about leaving, they vanished in that moment. I knew then that I was doing the right thing.

Although it seemed ludicrous at the time, I think back on that moment, and I feel compassion for her. What unhealed wound was she walking around with, what caused her to chase the spotlight so jealously? Even with our rivalry, any person seeking that much love and attention deserved my empathy and not my contempt. But I was too hurt to realize that yet.

Compassion is sparse for an infertile woman in this day and age, where baby making has become a competitive sport, a public spectacle. It's fine for the woman that is happily pregnant and open to sharing her adventure with those around her, but what about the rest of us? How does a woman dealing with repeated pregnancy loss navigate a world where the activity inside a woman's uterus is up for public commentary?

People make assumptions about a woman's fertility, they use her plight as leverage, they delight in her pain because it makes them believe that suffering chose her instead of them. Everyone supports the pregnant woman, but the woman who is going through fertility treatments has to carefully gauge who is on her team. Who among her friends is capable of helping, and who is only capable of hurting. But they all become part of the story.

CHAPTER 21

March, 2011

The freedom to work from home changed everything, I was thrilled to leave my toxic work environment behind. I felt isolated, working alone in my condo all day, but I was immediately less stressed. Slowly, I began to construct the life and routine I wanted.

One Sunday in March, I had popped over to the Whole Foods near our house to pick up a rotisserie chicken when I spotted a pet rescue group set up across the street showing dogs and cats available for adoption. I put the chicken in my car and went over to check them out.

Immediately, this fifteen-pound Dachshund mix found me. The volunteer told me his name was Clancy and suggested I take him for a short walk. I'd always wanted a dog, but with both of us working full-time jobs outside the house, the time had never been right to adopt one. Clancy was kind of a spazz, peeing on everything and frantically zig-zagging along the sidewalk, but there was something about this dog that felt right to me. I asked the volunteers a bunch of questions, and their answers made me feel like Clancy and I could be a good match.

I hurried home and dragged Nile away from his computer, nervous that if we didn't hurry back, someone else would adopt Clancy out from under us. Nile played with him a bit and gave his stamp of approval. I knew most of the work would be on me, and I was okay with that.

It turned out that Clancy required some training and TLC to overcome severe separation anxiety. I spent a lot of time caring for him before he got to the point where I could more or less resume my once-independent life. We lived in a glorious area of Santa Monica, where the ocean meets the mountains, and together we took daily walks winding down through the lush hillsides to the beach. I felt so lucky, like I'd broken out of jail.

I continued to see my acupuncturist, Dr. Zheng, weekly. She felt that I could get pregnant without IUI or IVF, so we tried for a natural conception for a while. I'd also begun to see a chiropractor. Somewhere in my online research, I'd read that chiropractors can help with fertility by keeping the spine in line and balancing the nervous system. I had a good friend whose sister-in-law couldn't get pregnant for many months until she visited a chiropractor and *wham-* she was pregnant! It was worth a shot.

Admittedly, I was a little nervous about seeing a chiropractor. I wasn't sure what they really did. In passing, I'd heard the term "quack" associated with the practice. And, in my twenties, I read an article in a women's magazine about a woman who had a stroke after a chiropractor twisted her neck too hard and tore an artery. It was worth a try, but I proceeded with caution.

Someone in my yoga community recommended Dr. Goldner, a chiropractor in our area who was covered by our insurance. I called his office and scheduled a consultation. When I checked in for my appointment, his office assistant took my paperwork, put me in an exam room, turned on a video and left the room.

The video was meant to explain the basics of chiropractic care to new patients, but it had this cult-ish "hippy" vibe that I just couldn't get past. I'd seen a zillion doctors for things a lot more complicated than chiropractic care, and none of them had ever asked me to sit down and watch a video. It gave me a weird feeling, but I kept reminding myself that this man was in my circle of wellness friends and came highly recommended. And maybe, just maybe, he would be the difference between baby and no baby.

Dr. Goldner came into the room a few minutes after the video ended. I gave him the same medical history speech that I gave every time I met a new doctor. I got a little teary when I described the early miscarriages. He was kind and warm and said he could help me. In fact, he said he'd helped other women conceive and if he "could hang a shingle out-side" advertising such services, he would. I could see the entrepreneurial wheels turning in his head more than I could see any earnestness for healing patients. I was glad to hear that he had success in this specific area, but I felt turned-off. Like my loss was his gain, and he liked it that way.

During his physical examination of my spine, he explained that I also needed a spinal x-ray to show what he couldn't see. He walked me down the hall to the x-ray room. I was a little hesitant to get the x-ray since we were trying to conceive. Would the x-ray of my spinal column fry my eggs? Not wanting to shut the door on something that could help me, I just went with it and let him do the x-ray.

Back in the exam room alone, his assistant came in with a clipboard. She asked me to pick my treatment plan from a menu of options. She said the doctor recommended coming in five days a week for a few weeks, then tapering down to three days and so on. *Five days a week?!*

She showed me the total cost for this plan, and it was about $3,000! Mind you, I didn't have any pain or injury, I was just there for overall wellness. At that point, I was thoroughly confused. I chose this doctor specifically because he was in-network with my insurance plan and my copay was $25 per visit. I'd have to come over a hundred times to rack up a $3,000 tab.

I explained that I just wanted to pay the copays for each appointment. She looked at me like I was the most frustrating person she'd ever encountered. It started to feel like a time-share pitch. I fought the urge to run out of the room. She asked me to sign the contract, stating that I would pay thousands of dollars for the treatment plan. I refused. We were in some sort of weird, unnecessary stand-off.

She left the room, and I was left alone like a child waiting in the principal's office. When Dr. Goldner came back in, I told him what I had told the nurse: that I didn't want to sign up for this kind of commitment and that coming in five days a week seemed excessive. I still lacked complete confidence in my instincts since I was completely new to chiropractic, but I had just enough gumption to communicate that I wasn't comfortable with the whole thing. He stated that my insurance may not cover very much, blah, blah, blah. But I knew that it was just a $25 copay to see him. I wasn't sure how much the x-ray would cost, but I told him I was willing to take my chances and let his office and the insurance company sort it out. He was visibly disappointed.

It didn't bode well that our doctor-patient relationship started with a battle. I'd seen dozens of doctors in the last five years, none were perfect people, but none made me feel like he did. I'd felt like cattle being herded from place to place before, but this time I felt like I was being truly manipulated.

At the end of our conversation, we agreed to take it one visit at a time and that his office would be compensated through my insurance company. *Phew. We have an agreement. Why did we have to go through all of that?*

Then, he asked if I wanted to have an adjustment during this visit. I wasn't sure I trusted him, it felt like he had just tried to take advantage of me and now he was asking if I wanted him to adjust my spine. I wasn't ready to go back to the chiropractic "drawing board" just yet, so I let him adjust my neck, spine, and hips. Later that evening, he called to make sure I was feeling well after the adjustment. It still felt weird, but maybe we'd gotten past it.

On the next visit, I decided to treat the first appointment as water under the bridge. He did pretty much the same adjustments each time, and I was in and out of there in ten minutes. I really did feel better, and continued to see him regularly for about five months. Despite the gimmicks, it seemed to be working for my body. I saw the chiropractor a couple dozen times over the next several months, and it only cost me $615 – a far cry from the original price tag.

Years later, I heard a chiropractor say "bad chiropractic is better than no chiropractic." I'm not sure if that's true, but it did make me think of my experience with Dr. Goldner. My intuition served me well in my interaction with him, and I would come to rely on it even more with the doctor that I saw next.

CHAPTER 22

For the next few months, my routine consisted of working for a few hours in the morning and then spending the rest of the day walking my dog, doing yoga, and going to acupuncture and chiropractic sessions. I felt better than ever, but I still wasn't pregnant. We went on a beautiful vacation to Kauai, I was happy and healthy in almost every way. But I wasn't pregnant. I felt like I'd given my homemade wellness plan a fair shot, but it was clear that I needed something more if I wanted to graduate from *healthy* to *fertile*.

After we returned from Kauai, I scheduled an appointment with a new OBGYN for my annual pap smear, having broken up with my previous doctor after she dismissed my infertility worries. I hoped this new doctor would have some answers for me, and if not she might at least order some of the tests and procedures on my list of things to try. That way I could get the tests covered by my insurance since pretty much everything at the fancy fertility clinic was paid for out-of-pocket.

My experience with the new OBGYN, Dr. Welch, was what I had come to expect from a standard appointment. She was empathetic to my infertility struggles, but referred me to an outside fertility clinic (the one I was already going to) for help.

Ugh, another dead end. I berated myself a little for entertaining a hope that this doctor would be the one with answers. *Why don't OBGYNs know anything about infertility? Why can't women get precursory testing and answers from a mainstream doctor before turning to a fertility doctor? Why is basic infertility diagnosis and treatment considered an optional, non-covered luxury?*

Meanwhile, time was running out for me to enjoy under-employment. My only lead was to go back to Dr. Silberman, the hot-shot fertility doctor, and see what he suggested we try next.

At my next appointment, Dr. Silberman didn't offer much guidance. He said I could go either way, which irked me a little bit. This was becoming a pattern with him, always leaving decisions up to me without offering the information I needed in order to make them. Although fertility is a huge personal decision – the money, the time, the emotional risks - I really wanted his expertise and his professional opinion.

Again, I felt like I was at the blackjack table in Las Vegas. *Do I "hit" or do I "hold"? Do I bet $2,000 for IUI, or $12,000 for IVF?*

We decided on IVF. With all of the appointments involved, it would be much easier to pull off while I wasn't fully employed. So many people had asked me over the last year or two if we had tried IVF yet. When I answered *no*, their response was always a version of, "Well, see, there's your answer." Maybe they were right.

For this cycle, I was on very different drugs to assist in egg production than I had been in my prior IUI cycles. Trying something new always renewed my sense of hope. When I received my large shipment of meds for the IVF cycle, I excitedly laid them all out on my bathroom counter. I took pictures of my haul of vials, syringes and other medical supplies, imagining the photo caption "Where babies come from, LOL." This was apparently how my baby would come into the world, and I was becoming more and more okay with that.

Going through IVF for the first time, I felt empowered and unafraid. Over the years, I'd spent so much time and energy resisting even the idea of IVF. I was scared of the needles and going under anesthesia. And, I'd been apprehensive about spending all that money with a slim chance of success. But once we made the decision to do it, I felt at peace.

Everything started off pretty smoothly. Dr. Silberman made some comments about how my follicles were developing, which I bookmarked in my mind to research later with Dr. Google. Because I had so much time on my hands, I was researching every little thing and making myself crazy in the process. I knew it was unhealthy, that I was bordering on obsession, so I purchased a guided meditation program for each day of my IVF cycle. It always delivered the exact message I needed, when I needed it, to help me stay calm.

One day, I headed out for a long walk with Clancy to clear my mind. Winding through the sidewalks of our neighborhood on our way to the beach, I met a new neighbor who was in her later years. She fussed over Clancy, commenting on how cute he was. Then she asked if I had any kids. I said *no*, and braced for her reply. "Good for you!" she said. "It's 2011 and the future seems so bad, who would raise children in this world?" I smiled. Even though I was pretty clear that I wanted kids, it was refreshing to hear something other than the usual "pity" response that I'd heard a thousand times.

In fact, I wanted kids precisely so that when I was her age, I would feel the fullness of life, the optimism and love and support that you get from having a family. The world *is* a crazy place, but what would make it worth living? When I enter my 50s, I want to be sending kids off to college. When I welcome my 60s, I want to hear all about their careers, their love interests and how they are navigating the world on their own. I want my world to get bigger as I age, and my life fuller.

At our next appointment with Dr. Silberman, we learned that I was not making as many eggs as he would have liked. And, it looked like one follicle was growing faster than the others. I didn't have enough eggs to warrant the cost and effort of IVF, so the cycle was converted to another IUI. While I was disappointed that IVF still eluded us, I was happy that we had bailed on an IVF when the odds were too low, saving us lots of money.

After the IUI, around the time implantation was expected to occur, I felt a stabbing pain in my back, on the right side. I also felt a sensation on the side of my neck that felt like my thyroid was straining. I experienced an effusive runny nose and other extreme allergy-like symptoms for the remaining five days of the cycle. Then, the symptoms abruptly stopped and my period came. *OMG, did I just miscarry again? On this janky IVF turned IUI cycle?*

I wasn't taking any home pregnancy tests during this cycle, so I didn't have any concrete evidence. But the symptoms were too familiar for me to believe it was anything else.

This was getting old.

CHAPTER 23

After the IVF-turned-IUI cycle failed, it was time to take a step back. It didn't feel right to continue down what felt like a dead-end road. We had been through seven IUI's so far, in addition to a long list of other interventions, only to be left with the same outcome - early miscarriage.

Dr. Silberman said that it wasn't necessarily a bad sign that these IUIs hadn't worked. It was just bad luck. Or, more accurately, it was statistically improbable that it would work. That was one of the hardest things to wrap my brain around - we were paying a ton of money for something that probably wouldn't work! He said we were too young for genetics to be a factor.

I was beginning to form the opinion that my body was fighting off the embryos when they implanted, like an allergic reaction. It seemed a little crazy and far-fetched, and every doctor blew me off when I shared this theory with them. I believed that Dr. Silberman was doing his best, but there was something else going on that he couldn't solve. There were questions in the back of my mind that wouldn't stop nagging me. I had no clue where I would find the answers, but I wasn't done looking either.

Still stuffy from the intense allergy symptoms of the previous cycle, I treated myself to a massage in hopes that it would help me feel better. As my masseuse, Olivia, led me into the treatment room, I felt obligated to assure her that I wasn't actually sick or contagious, even though I sounded like it. She was relieved and said that it was unbelievable how often people booked massage appointments when they were sick to help them feel better, putting her at risk for illness and income loss. As she worked the tension out of my muscles, I shared some of our infertility journey and my suspicions that my body was fighting off my pregnancies.

Talking to Olivia was so easy, like chatting with a longtime friend. She recommended that I see a chiropractor, suggesting the same one I'd previously worked with. I laughed and said, "Yeah I used to see him." Her lack of advice was a let-down, I realized that I'd actually hoped that Olivia had something tangible for me to go on. *Do I actually think a masseuse has the key to my fertility? Am I getting that desperate? Who will I consult next, the barista at the coffee shop?*

As I lay on the table, berating myself, Olivia put a bug in my ear to get my "levels checked" for my adrenals and allergies. She had previously worked for a natural chiropractor in Northern California, and those were the common things he would test in women experiencing infertility. She promised to send me more information if I left a note at the front desk with my email address.

Something about her suggestion struck a chord with me. Adrenal fatigue was one of the conditions on my radar, but I'd never explored it. I had always suspected that something was going on with my hormones, because of my spotting, but the tests had always come back normal. However, I had never considered food allergy testing. I'd been tested as a kid because I had chronic ear infections and the test results showed that I was basically allergic to everything. My mom tried to avoid all of the trigger-foods, but it was next to impossible, and she didn't have much incentive to follow through. Ear infections aside, I was a pretty happy and healthy kid.

I checked out of the spa feeling much more optimistic than when I had walked in. I made sure to leave Olivia a generous tip and scribbled my email address on the envelope.

In all the years of facing infertility, my most powerful ally was always the undying seeds of hope. Like a weed, hope sprang up fresh and green in unexpected places, at unexpected times, no matter how often it had been attacked and seemingly destroyed. Even as I lay on a massage table, sick and tired and empty, there it was – a tiny sprout of hope, reaching out to the person nearest me.

I still marvel at the fact that a woman I've only seen once in my life for 50 minutes was the person who started me down the road that would ultimately lead to my children.

CHAPTER 24

November, 2011

For my entire life as far back as I could remember, I've had stomach problems. It was so common that I had never thought of it as a "medical condition," per se. It was just the way I was - I had brown eyes and stomach problems. Knowing what I know now, I suspect they were caused by the overuse of antibiotics to treat my childhood chronic ear infections.

My issues weren't as debilitating as irritable bowel syndrome, I would just get stomach aches sometimes and generally felt burpy or gassy when I ate. Once in a while, I would need to lie down after a meal, massaging my tummy until it was less uncomfortable.

The Celiac Disease tests that I had requested years before had all come back negative, so I knew it wasn't a gluten allergy. Things improved as my diet became healthier, but it was like my symptoms had been dialed down - still there, just quieter. I would still experience stomach pain, even after eating healthy foods like salad, and had no idea why.

Following my massage with Olivia, I Googled "naturopaths" and what I learned resonated with me. I knew that my primary care physician wasn't going to figure out whether my tendency to be burpy was related to my infertility. I considered seeing a dietitian, but that didn't seem right either. I already knew a lot about nutrition.

So, I did what every responsible consumer of healthcare should do. I searched Yelp for a naturopath. I found a listing for a smiling Dr. Macky, a naturopath near me who had good reviews. Some of the reviewers left pretty detailed feedback about their experiences - enough to make me feel comfortable choosing her.

At my first appointment, Dr. Macky and I spoke for over an hour about my medical history, specifically our infertility. She was warm and empathetic to my struggles, yet unfazed by my problems – which sparked a hope in me that she might have answers. I wondered if this is what doctor-patient relationships used to be like, the doctor taking the time to ask questions, digging deeper and deeper into the issue. She was doing a thorough intake instead of just blurting out "You are young and healthy and fine!" like most doctors.

We discussed my entire medical background, and she suggested that we test for food allergies, micronutrients (vitamins and minerals) and heavy metals. This energized me. *New tests, maybe new answers!*

At the end of our conversation, and without much fanfare, she handed me a binder. She gave all of her patients this binder to hold test results, food journals and the materials she created for them. It was pre-filled with information that would be relevant to me, as well as a "Conception Regimen" for me to implement on my own. The gesture made me feel like I mattered, that my health information was important to her and that we'd work together toward improving my health.

Dr. Macky drew two vials of blood and sent them to two specialty labs. The first was a food allergy test that measured immunoglobulin G (IgG) antibodies. The test results show whether a patient has a low, moderate or high reaction to 190 different foods. The second blood test measured the presence of vitamins and minerals at the cellular level to identify any deficiencies. She also gave me a take-home urine test for heavy metals.

The results took about a month to come back. While I waited, I reviewed the Conception Regimen. It included a lot of information that I'd come across before in my research.

Some of them were things I'd already experimented with, but not consistently. It's hard to be your own guinea pig, especially when there is a never-ending list of things to try.

For example, I decided to be better about taking a regular probiotic. I also tried to improve the length and quality of my sleep. I started taking fish oil again. And, I gave a castor oil pack a try (to reduce uterine stagnation). A month later, I practically skipped into her office to get the results, positive that helpful answers were waiting for me.

First, we reviewed the food allergy test results. I'd always thought that either you were allergic to a food, or you weren't. I didn't know "food sensitivity" was a thing - an actual scientific *thing*. I thought food sensitivities were products of the imagination, something invented by high-maintenance picky eaters. We reviewed the report together, highlighting the foods I was sensitive to.

That report contained the most helpful information I'd received in the last four years, perhaps ever. Some of the foods that came back as highly reactive were not a surprise, like dairy. I've always been sensitive to dairy, but it wasn't a full-blown allergy, so I still ate some here and there. However, the tests did show that I was far less sensitive to goat's milk. Almonds were also on the list. Because cow's milk had never sat well with me, the dairy alternative I used daily was almond milk. Turned out, my body was reacting to almonds, but I hadn't connected the dots. *Looks like somebody's switching to goat's milk from now on.*

Based on the test results, I was pretty clear now on what not to eat – cow's milk and dairy, malt/gluten, egg whites, almonds, kale, pineapple, kidney beans, navy beans, green beans, vanilla, and garlic. Looking at the list, some of my seemingly random stomach aches started to make sense. Dr. Macky's plan was to avoid these foods completely for a month and then add them back in one by one to see how I reacted.

The test for heavy metals showed no issue with metals in my system. Then we talked about the other blood test, the one that measured the vitamin and mineral content of my blood cells. It showed that I was deficient in B12 and Coenzyme Q10, both of which are critical for egg quality and embryo development. It was surprising that I was deficient in B12 since I ate a lot of meat. I soon learned that deficiencies aren't always an issue of not consuming enough, they can also be the result of an unhealthy gut not absorbing the nutrients in food properly. Or, they can be caused by a genetic condition. (Around this time, I was also diagnosed with a fertility genetic deal-breaker called MTHFR.*)

Dr. Macky put together a regimen of supplements that would fill in the gaps where I was missing essential nutrients. It was a beautiful plan, a blend of science and intuition. My "baby binder" was filling up with exciting, helpful information. For the first time, I felt like I was on to something.

Once I stripped all of the reactive foods from my diet, I was basically left with fruit, veggies, and meat. I joking dubbed my diet "vegan but with meat." Thankfully, since my diet closely resembled the paleo diet, there were a ton of blogs, cookbooks and recipe ideas out there to inspire me and keep me (and my husband) fed.

After a few months on my version of the paleo diet, I took it a step further by going on something called the Autoimmune Protocol (AIP). In this protocol, you also eliminate additional highly reactive foods like eggs, nuts, seeds, coffee, chocolate, nightshades (tomatoes, eggplants, potatoes, peppers), alcohol and a number of other foods considered to be unfriendly to the gut. I charged forward and gave up these foods, too.

Honestly, I wasn't perfect about it. Everything I read said that you needed to be wholly committed to it, and I do understand the reasons behind that. However, I just found it impossible to be perfect while maintaining a normal work and social life. I also don't like the idea that something has to be 100% perfect or it will fail. I just don't buy that. I'd say I was probably 90% dilligent about sticking to the AIP.

One of the best resources I found on the science behind the paleo diet and autoimmunity was Dr. Sarah Ballantyne, also known as "The Paleo Mom."* Through her work, I learned more about the connection between gut health and overall health. I sought out her research on "leaky gut syndrome," which happens when the intestines become permeable and tiny particles escape, triggering attacks by the immune system. Whether leaky gut syndrome is embraced by western medicine or not, it is understood that the good bacteria in our intestines calms the immune system.

My overarching goal was to reduce immune responses of any kind. I was beginning to suspect that my early miscarriages were due to an overactive immune system. Eventually, western medical results would confirm this hypothesis. For now, armed with the results of my blood tests, I felt like I was finally in control. I couldn't stop my body from having allergies, but I could eliminate allergy triggers by controlling what went into my mouth.

I had dabbled with being gluten-free once before and couldn't do it. But I had acted on a vague idea that it was better for me. Those instincts turned out to be right, and now I had proof. Nothing motivates me more than cold, hard facts that back up my intuition.

CHAPTER 25

I was hoping that by changing my diet I could somehow cure my infertility, but I knew better than to count on it.

Once I started following my naturopath's protocol, the protocol from my acupuncturist began to feel obsolete. Although I very much respected Dr. Zheng for helping some of my friends conceive, I had lost confidence in her ability to help me. I started dragging my feet when it was time to schedule another appointment. At $200 per visit, my wallet wasn't happy either. After almost a year, the daily charting and horrible tasting teas didn't seem worth it anymore. I had no doubt she was skilled, I just needed someone else.

Through my Resolve support group, I heard about an acupuncturist in my neighborhood who was "getting everybody pregnant." Turned out, he was in-network for my insurance plan, so I would only have to pay a $20 copay to see him. Many "infertility" acupuncturists are at least $150 per session, including Chinese herbs. *Could the answer to my prayers be this man who's been under my nose this whole time?*

I headed to his office on Abbot Kinney Boulevard (the self-proclaimed "hippest street in America") to see what all the fuss was about. Dr. Hoff was extremely gentle and sincere. I felt really comfortable in his hands. His approach was more about general wellness, not specifically infertility. Since I'd just come from the serious infertility acupuncturist, this was a nice change of pace. He gave me his cheat sheet with tips for a healthy diet and lifestyle. Many of the things he mentioned were things I was either already doing or was interested in learning about. But a few were new, and I was excited to add those to my infinite list of "things to try." We were on the same page.

During his needle treatment, I became so relaxed that I always fell asleep. I slept so deeply that I'd wake up with a start, wondering where the hell I was. I'd never felt that way during acupuncture before. During one particular evening appointment, I settled onto the table as the sun's final rays streamed in through the skylights and windows. When I woke up, it was completely dark in the office. I panicked and thought he'd forgotten that I was on the table with needles all over me. *What if he locked up the office and went home?*

I imagined myself getting up from the table, partially dressed with all these needles sticking out of me, and breaking out of the office through the glass door. I'd look like some kind of acupuncture zombie. Just as I was getting up the courage to get off the table and find my way out, Dr. Hoff came in to remove the needles and sent me on my way.

Each week, I looked forward to my appointment with him. We chatted easily about our spouses and other things going on in our life. If we had met some other way, I was sure we would become good friends. I wasn't sure what effect he was having on my fertility, but I could tell that he was increasing my general wellbeing. If nothing else, I always got a very restorative nap, and it only cost me $20.

CHAPTER 26

Dr. Macky legitimized the stomach issues I'd experienced over the years when mainstream doctors had left me high and dry. Between my drastic diet changes and the healing hands of Dr. Hoff, my body felt free, clean and capable as ever.

I found it ironic that four years into my infertility struggle, I had better overall well-being than ever before. Everything I was learning about my body and how to live healthier might have stayed a mystery forever if we had been able to have babies right away.

We continued trying to conceive naturally, but my pregnancy symptoms always evaporated quickly. Regular drugstore pregnancy tests aren't able to detect pregnancy until after the first day of a woman's missed period, but my symptoms were always fading away by then. I finally got tired of *wondering* if I was pregnant and decided it was time to know for sure. I had been angry at my doctors for ignoring my intuition, but wasn't I ignoring it too by not proving it? If we were going to be scientific about solving my infertility, then my miscarriages needed to be either confirmed once and for all, or removed from the equation.

I went online and ordered a package of high-sensitivity pregnancy tests that can detect pregnancy a week sooner than regular drug store tests, and started using them every time I felt pregnant.

And there it was, spelled out in neat, pink lines. The first tangible evidence that my suspicions were right. I *was* getting pregnant, but I wasn't staying pregnant.

If that was the case, then infertility treatments to *get* me pregnant weren't doing any better than trying naturally. All of the plumbing was working. My body was allowing the embryo to form and to implant. It was after implantation that something was going haywire. None of my fertility treatments had addressed that problem at all. I had never seen a treatment option that did.

A woman in my Resolve support group named Sarah had shared her experience working remotely with a Reproductive Immunologist (RI) in another part of the country. I was fascinated to learn that Reproductive Immunology is an obscure field of study that focuses on why pregnancies are rejected. She recommended the book Is Your Body Baby Friendly? by Alan E. Beer, MD.* Reading it gave me all these pings of recognition. *Yes! Yes! Yes! This is what is happening to me.*

The book was a bit technical, but it thoroughly explained the decades of research behind Dr. Beer's practice and methodology. This wasn't some experimental voodoo, this was science.

What I remember about Sarah's story was a blur of crazy interventions, IV drips and trips to Mexico for a treatment that was banned in the US. This was definitely the road less traveled, and I wasn't sure I wanted to take it. In fact, I was convinced that I did not. On the surface, it seemed crazy. But I knew that this woman was definitely not crazy. She was informed, methodical.

Like me.

CHAPTER 27

O nce I realized that my fertility problems fell outside the realm of *common* fertility solutions, I had to start considering *uncommon* solutions. Even though the idea of working with a Reproductive Immunologist appealed to me, I hesitated.

How much is this going to cost?

How long will it take to go through the treatment plan and be cleared to cycle?

What terrible thing are they going to find?

What if I do all those crazy things and it still doesn't work?

I sat on it for a while, hoping that something would save me from having to decide which way to turn. A sign, or a sudden medical breakthrough, or a miraculous natural pregnancy.

Then, one November evening, after drinking a glass of wine and contemplating my infertility, I filled out the online patient intake forms for the RI clinic. *Here we go again,* I thought: recapping my medical history, requesting charts, files, scans and x-rays from every doctor I'd ever seen. The baby binder was getting a workout. A few days after I submitted the forms, the clinic sent me an email with a long list of tests they required me to have done.

I ran around town getting more than twenty vials of blood drawn at different labs for different tests. That part was easy. The RI also wanted an endometrial biopsy to test my uterine cells for deficiencies. The problem was, I did not have an OBGYN that I could ask to perform the biopsy. I had broken up with my previous OBGYN because she had been so dismissive about my fertility concerns. I had only seen my new OBGYN, Dr. Welch, once for an annual exam, and she also did not demonstrate a willingness to help me solve the issue of my recurrent miscarriages. It felt awkward to call her up and ask her to perform an endometrial biopsy just because some out-of-town doctor wanted me to have one. But we couldn't move forward without it.

Dr. Welch's nurse was thoroughly confused when I called to make the appointment. Our medical system isn't set up for patients to call in and request a procedure that the doctor hasn't ordered, and for good reason. After some explaining and insistence from me, she agreed to make an appointment for me to see the doctor.

Going into Dr. Welch's office that day, I anticipated that I would spend this visit talking her into it and then have to schedule a follow-up appointment for the actual biopsy. On the off-chance that we did the procedure that day, I asked Nile to come with me for support.

When Dr. Welch came into the exam room, her helpful attitude eased my nerves a little. I explained that I was working remotely with a Reproductive Immunologist to help me get to the bottom of my miscarriages, and an endometrial biopsy was part of the intake diagnostic process. I produced for her the lab slip with the shipping and handling information for the biopsy specimen.

She glanced down at the piece of paper in my hand, then looked up at me with an angry, stunned glare. I tried to explain why I was pursuing this line of treatment, but it was as if I was speaking a foreign language. She said there was no reason to do an endometrial biopsy related to infertility or miscarriages. She also dismissed the field of Reproductive Immunology as a whole. Not only did she not support my initiative, she was angry that I even approached her with this.

I didn't get it. Okay, so doctors don't typically like to work with other doctors who they don't know, and don't take kindly to being told what to do. I really tried to frame my request under a we-are-all-in-this-together-to-solve-my-crisis-of-babies-dying-in-my-uterus appeal. But she was unmoved. I couldn't understand why she found my request so foreign and offensive.

There are plenty of peer-reviewed studies of Reproductive Immunology treatments. Many women have endometrial biopsies, or endometrial scratches, to increase their chances of conception after repeated miscarriages. How did I know all of this and she didn't? I understand that doctors prefer to see a mountain of evidence before implementing a treatment, but by the time they have gathered enough evidence I will be in my 50s. It will be too late.

Sitting in the exam room, I felt the incredible burden of having to beg for help. I felt so vulnerable to be presenting my case to a doctor who was trying to shut the door in my face, essentially telling me I was crazy.

These moments were some of the hardest for me. I knew I was repeatedly miscarrying, and I felt like nobody cared. We live in a world where terms like "family first" and "pro-life" abound, but a baby dying spontaneously in a woman's body...*meh.* My interactions with skeptical doctors with their who-knows-why-anyone-miscarries attitudes made me feel like I was the problem, bothering them with my "petty" worries when they had real issues to deal with.

By now, I wasn't just going on my suspicions. I had real proof of my miscarriages, proof that any doctor would respect. What baffled me was that every specialist I had worked with wasn't trying to determine the cause and put a stop to the miscarriages. My OBGYNs just acted like it wasn't happening, that it would just magically stop someday. And my fertility doctors just wanted me to keep trying IUIs or IVF without investigating why my pregnancies didn't last.

That was the moment when it all came to a head. I had just about had enough. If I could scrape my own uterus I would, but I couldn't. I wasn't going to let this doctor decide that I couldn't pursue this option. If she wouldn't do it, I'd find someone else who would.

I came within half a second of telling her so, but right then she grudgingly consented to perform the biopsy. She must have concluded that if I was crazy enough to saunter into her office and request that she scrape my uterus real quick, I must be serious. And she was right about that.

She sighed and huffed and puffed as we discussed the details of where to send the specimen, etc. Throughout all this, Nile didn't say a word. He didn't know anything about the procedure, he was just there for moral support and to help me afterward if I was in pain. But I think his presence was what tipped the scale in our favor. If I was alone, she could easily have written me off as crazy. But I wasn't alone - I had the full support of my rational, level-headed husband. Much harder to dismiss *both* of us as crazy.

The biopsy lasted only seconds, but ten seconds of feeling my insides being scraped with a knife was almost unbearable. This was like pap smear discomfort times a million. But then it was over, and I was okay. As I left that office, I thought *I'm one step closer to figuring this out.*

That was the last time I ever saw that doctor.

CHAPTER 28

January, 2012

After completing all of the required blood work and the endometrial biopsy, it was time to set up my phone consultation with Dr. Peres, the Reproductive Immunologist. When I called to make the appointment, the nurse was enthusiastic and wanted to get me scheduled a.s.a.p. Her tone was slightly congratulatory, almost like "you made it this far - twenty vials of blood drawn and sent out to three different labs *and* you got your uterus scraped out - you may pass GO and collect $200!"

I received all my test results a few days ahead of my consult and spent the better part of my days searching the Reproductive Immunology Support Yahoo! message board, trying to interpret them myself so that I'd be prepared for our brief meeting. There were pages and pages of blood test results, everything from typical CBC results to genetic markers that were previously unknown to me.

I went line by line through all of my results and highlighted anything I wanted to ask the doctor about. By the time we had our appointment, I had practically completed a crash course in Reproductive Immunology.

During our initial phone consult, Dr. Peres efficiently reviewed my test results and laid out his proposed treatment plan. He explained that I needed to start taking an extra folic acid supplement right away and take a blood thinner when trying to conceive. I was also a little bit hypothyroid, so he added a prescription for a low dose of thyroid meds.

Moving on to the more specialized tests, the results showed that I did not have enough protective cells to allow the embryo to successfully implant. *Finally, a test result that proved my theory!*

The treatment for this problem was something called Lymphocyte Immune Therapy, or LIT. One particular test revealed that my immune system was generally overactive, and steroids were needed to suppress it. It was pretty much what I expected, but it was still a lot to take in. Steroids, blood thinners and LIT, oh my! *I'm definitely not in Kansas anymore.*

Answers! I had answers! My "unexplained infertility" finally had an *explanation.*

Dr. Peres said that his practice had a 70% success rate, whereas without the treatment my chances of having a baby were less than 10 percent. I took his assessment with a grain of salt, of course, but I knew my odds of conceiving without any intervention were extremely low. I'd already proven that. I liked that he was so nonchalant. "You have this issue, and this is how we'll treat it." It was all laid out in black and white.

I felt like someone had finally figured me out because they bothered to look.

The process of being "cleared to cycle" would take a couple of months. The most involved and time-consuming treatment would be the LIT procedure.

An embryo is a foreign object to the mother's body because its genetic material is not identical to the mother's. In some cases, a woman's body lacks enough defense cells (or "LAD's") to protect the embryo from the immune system, which then attacks the embryo as if it were a disease.

LIT is a pretty simple intervention, rudimentary in fact. It involves drawing blood from the "donor" which is usually the intended father. The blood is spun to isolate the white blood cells, which are then injected under the skin on the forearm of the intended mother. The woman's immune system learns to recognize the DNA in the new cells, and the desired results are that LADs go up and the body is now able to protect the embryo.

This treatment basically tells the body, "Hey, you see these cells from the father? Next time you see them in the uterus, recognize it as a friend and not a foe. Protect it." It immunizes the body similarly to how a vaccine works. LIT can also help lower "natural killer" (NK) cells, which my test results showed were slightly elevated.

I knew that embryos were implanting in my uterus and quickly failing. I knew that pregnancy felt like an allergy, like my body wasn't happy about the embryo being there. Maybe the crux of my problem was a matter of arranging the proper introductions between my immune system and Nile's DNA. My gut told me that the LIT procedure was worth a shot.

The biggest hurdle to get over with regard to LIT therapy was not the out of pocket cost, but the minor issue of it being banned in the US.

We'd already spent thousands of dollars on years of failed fertility treatments. Now, we were about to go down this immunology road that was going to cost us a lot more, both financially and emotionally, with no guarantee. Oh, and I would have to go to Mexico twice to complete the treatment. I felt fear creeping up and tried my best to tamp it down.

I'm a cynical person by nature. If something is banned, I don't immediately write it off. But I did want to know *why* LIT therapy was banned. I had heard through the grapevine that before the ban it was performed at many of the major hospitals in Los Angeles, like UCLA, Cedars Sinai, and even my own fertility clinic.

The FDA banned LIT in 2002. The reason (as I understood it) was that the FDA classifies the use of blood cells from the father under the same umbrella as stem cell research, which was highly restricted at the time. The FDA requires the blood product used in LIT to be treated like a drug and go through the approval process like any new drug or treatment. Since LIT relies on the transfer of fresh blood cells from the father to the mother, these restrictions effectively halted the use of it in the US.

The decision whether or not to do the LIT treatment was hard, and I drew upon all the resources I had. I had the personal experience of a friend. I had the stories and testimonials women shared on the RI Support message board. I read the studies and the FDA letter that explained the ban. I asked the doctor if LIT was required, and he felt strongly that it would be an effective treatment for me but understood that not everyone is comfortable with it. Some people choose not to do it because of the ban, some can't stomach the idea of getting medical treatment in Mexico, and others just opt out for logistical reasons. Lots of people get pregnant without doing LIT.

For my friend from the Resolve support group, LIT was the magic bullet. She credited it as the most effective intervention that led to her successful pregnancy. She and almost anyone else would agree that there's definitely an element of the unknown at play when it comes to fertility. Most of us will never know exactly how our infertility was resolved, but there's a lot you can learn through trial and error.

At the Resolve support group, I learned a lot from other people's experiences, especially when they shared what they believed worked for them. It's anecdotal, of course; not exactly what you'd call double-blind scientific studies. But I listened when they spoke. I made mental and physical notes, all of which would be crucial down the road.

Honestly, LIT therapy itself didn't seem that controversial once I had all the information. But I did have a nagging "wait, is this crazy?" feeling. I researched myself down the rabbit hole and back, and eventually decided in favor of the treatment. I didn't want to have any regrets. Luckily, my husband was willing to do anything I was willing to do. He knew I was as well informed as a non-medical professional could be.

CHAPTER 29

March, 2012

Lymphocyte Immunization Therapy is performed in Nogales, Mexico, on the US border near Tucson by a Mexican OBGYN named Dr. Sanchez. If I understood correctly, he and his wife were once patients of Dr. Beer when they had trouble conceiving, and they were successful under his immune treatments. So, when LIT was banned in the US, Dr. Sanchez set up shop on the weekends in Nogales, six hours from his weekday practice, to perform LIT on mostly US and Canadian patients.

I emailed Dr. Sanchez's assistant to make an appointment. She replied with a list of available dates, crucial information involving the process, and the price tag - $600. I booked round-trip plane tickets to Tucson for the weekend that worked best with Nile's schedule. The driver employed by the doctor would pick us up at the McDonald's in Nogales on the US side of the border. It was all set.

So, while our friends were going to the beach or watching college basketball, we were going to Mexico for secret fertility treatments. I decided not to tell my parents so they wouldn't worry about my safety. We didn't tell any of our friends, either. If you aren't informed, it's too much to wrap your brain around. Plus, most of our friends and family had no idea about the miscarriages. It was too hard to wind all that back and tell the whole story just to explain why we were about to board a plane to Arizona.

Thus, on a beautiful spring Saturday afternoon, we found ourselves driving through the Arizona desert to meet Eduardo, our driver, at McDonald's. We slipped the McDonald's parking attendant a few dollars to park in the lot for the day. Nile and I sat at an outside table taking in the sights and sounds of this bustling border town. Fairly quickly, I pegged a man and a woman at an adjacent table as another LIT couple. We struck up a conversation while we waited for our rendezvous at 4:00. Their friendliness and normalness took the edge off my nerves. *Normal, smart people are doing the same thing I'm doing,* I told myself. *This can't be that crazy.*

Soon, I spotted another potential LIT couple by the door of the restaurant. They looked as if they were having some sort of domestic dispute, but I wasn't sure. They were noticeably flashy, especially for a border town. Well-dressed and moneyed, like a society couple who lived on a ranch, they looked picture perfect, but something about the husband's behavior seemed off. He was a large man, and he kept going in and out of the McDonald's, causing a scene in the restaurant and then coming outside to rage at his wife and the town car driver they'd hired for their trip to the border. She seemed embarrassed, alternating between ignoring him and trying to corral him.

On the other hand, crazy people are also doing the same thing we're doing.

About twenty minutes past 4:00 pm, Eduardo pulled up in a gold tinted, late model minivan. He got out, gave us a warm greeting, and invited us to board the van. The Cowboy insisted on sitting in the front seat and chatted up Eduardo as we headed toward the border crossing. He was slurring his words and talking endlessly, like a drunken frat boy catching a cab to the after party. He expressed his displeasure with the car we were in, and Eduardo tried to change the subject by asking us where we were all from. The Cowboy replied that he and his wife were from Canada, and then he whipped out a fat wad of U.S. dollars to show the driver what a high-roller he was. I couldn't believe we were captive in a minivan crossing into Mexico with this idiot.

Oh my God, he is going to get us killed, I thought. So far, I had only calculated the risks of the LIT treatment itself, not the risks of traveling with mentally unstable strangers. Suddenly, the whole situation *did* seem kind of crazy.

The total time it took to get from McDonald's to the office was twenty minutes, including the time it took to cross the border. The office was so close that it would have been faster to walk. I imagined that I could scream and the U.S. Border Patrol would hear me and come to my aid. That's what I told myself, anyway. Before we left home, I had printed out copies of the address and walking directions to the office and back just in case we missed the pickup from McDonald's. I also printed out the address and directions to the nearest hospital on the US side in case of emergency. I was prepared. *My Dad would be proud. Actually, no. He would be incensed if he knew.*

Eduardo pulled the van into a parking spot on the side of a nondescript office building and walked us down the sidewalk, inside and up the stairs to Dr. Sanchez's office. We filed in, and each took a seat in the waiting room while Dr. Sanchez and his assistant gave us the rundown for the day, which looked something like this: The men ("donors") will have their blood drawn, one by one. Then, Eduardo will take us all to a local restaurant for an early dinner while they spin the blood and prepare it for injection. Then, we'll come back, the women ("patients") will receive the injections, and we will be on our merry way. The Canadian Cowboy couple had apparently been through this rodeo before, but it was the first time for the rest of us.

While Nile waited for his turn to have his blood drawn, I wrote in my journal. Mrs. Cowboy buried her nose in a book, ignoring everyone else. Her husband paced around anxiously, making us all aware of his looming, neurotic presence. After all of the "donors" were through, we followed Eduardo back to the minivan. The Canadian Cowboy Couple elected to go to a bar a few doors down from the doctor's office instead of joining us for dinner. So Nile and I found ourselves alone with the Normal Couple on the weirdest double-date ever.

Eduardo drove us up into the hills above Nogales and through the gated entrance of an upscale, traditional Mexican restaurant. We were the only people there. The men were hungry because they'd been fasting all day, and our collective anxiety had melted into the invigorating calm of waiting for the final step.

I ordered enchiladas and a Diet Coke and continued our earlier conversations with our new fertility tourist friends. Where do you live? (Toronto) What do you do for a living? (They both wrote algorithms to outsmart the American stock exchange.) What treatments have we done? Am I a bad fertility patient for drinking Diet Coke? It's the good kind here in Mexico, right? We made the kind of small talk you make when you are forced to spend a lot of time with people you don't know. But the food was great, and Nile enjoyed his Tecate. It almost felt normal. Infertility is like being thrust into a secret club that no one wants to be a member of. It's very isolating, and any camaraderie feels good, however fleeting.

After we finished eating and paid the bill, Eduardo arrived at our table and informed us that it was time to head back to the office. On the return drive, we were treated to a beautiful desert sunset- a watercolor sky flushed with orange, pink and purple.

As we pulled into the parking spot, the energy of the town had noticeably shifted in our absence. Nogales was beginning to come alive - a border town on a Saturday night. Businesses that were shuttered during the day were now open and ready to receive American tourists, many of them students from the University of Arizona. At the bar across the street from the clinic, a blonde college-aged girl was sitting atop a burro with a Dos Equis in one hand, pretending to ride it as if it were a bull, while her friend snapped pictures. She noticed the middle-aged healthcare tourists looking at her and smirked. I thought, *Girl, this might be you in fifteen years. Don't judge!*

The Canadian Cowboy Couple was already in the waiting room when we filed back in. Mr. Cowboy had apparently been drinking his ass off while we were gone and also purchased himself a new leather jacket with fringe detail and an oversized cowboy hat to match. He wore his new apparel like a costume over the clothes he was wearing. He was more inebriated and more annoying than before. They had finished their LIT treatment and were impatiently waiting for us.

My name was called first. We sat across the desk from the doctor while his nurse stood nearby, preparing the needles and supplies. Among the supplies were two syringes (one for each arm) filled with a clear liquid. The doctor cleaned the tender skin on my forearms with alcohol, and the nurse made four injections in the pattern of a square on each one. My mind was focused on wrapping up and getting the heck out of there, so I was unprepared for how much each injection hurt. I thought I'd conquered injections. Being injected eight times was like getting eight flu shots or eight bee stings. By the time she finished, my arms felt useless, like I'd been beaten up.

The nurse covered each injection site with a little round bandage. I stood up slowly, walked back to the waiting room, and sat down. Nile was at the front desk settling the bill and other paperwork. I started to feel nauseous, light headed. I had the overwhelming feeling that I was going to vomit.

I walked out of the office and started wandering down the hallway, looking for a bathroom. Eduardo came after me, probably uncomfortable with one of his charges wandering away. I told him I needed a bathroom and I could tell by his reaction that he understood what I meant. He said he would go get the key and hurried off. At this point, my strength had drained so much that I was leaning on a pillar in the hallway to hold myself up. Next thing I know, there's a big commotion and concerned voices and I am on the ground looking up at the ceiling. I had passed out. Luckily, Nile had just come out to check on me and caught me as I fell.

Eduardo, who had been right at his heels with the bathroom key, helped Nile carry me through the waiting room and back into the exam room. As I passed the other couples in the waiting room, a horrified look came over the face of the Normal Couple wife, who was up next to receive her injections. They laid me down on a table with my feet in the air. Nile said that I was very pale and sweating, that I could barely hear, see or function.

As soon as they got my feet up, I quickly began to feel better. Everyone around me was so concerned, which made me feel very cared for. Dr. Sanchez explained that sometimes the body's defense system kicks in and collapses the blood flow. Even in my groggy state, I wondered out loud if this was a clue about my overactive immune system, but he said that passing out didn't have anything to do with autoimmune issues. I didn't know what to make of it.

I continued to rest while the remaining patient got her injections. Before she went in, I reassured her that I was fine. She received the shots and immediately had the exact same reaction! I don't know if it was psychological or what, but she passed out just like I had. We each took a few more minutes to recover before the doctor felt comfortable releasing us.

Meanwhile, the Canadian Cowboy Couple was almost beside themselves for being stuck with us. I would say that the feeling was mutual, but at that point, I couldn't care less. I just wanted out of there.

For the last time, Eduardo herded us into the van, politely suggesting that the drunk Cowboy sit in the very back seat so as not to draw unnecessary attention at the border crossing. Apparently, nobody had ever told him to sit in the back of anything, but his wife finally convinced him to comply. The crossing back into the US was slower, but it was less crowded at night than during the day.

When we reached the guard station, the US Border Patrol agent asked what we were doing in Mexico while he reviewed our passports. We said, "we are here for a medical procedure." He shined his flashlight inside the car, looking at each of our faces. I just knew that when he got to Cowboy, we were done for. But to our surprise, he waved us through. Within seconds we were back at McDonald's, four hours after we had left.

The one-hour trip back to Tuscon gave Nile and I some time to decompress and discuss the ordeal. He was more freaked out about the whole experience than I was. It was harder for him to witness to my reaction to LIT than it was for me to experience it. He said that his life flashed before his eyes when he saw me collapse right in front of him. He imagined having to call my parents and tell them that I had died or was gravely ill due to some crazy-ass fertility treatment we were undergoing in Mexico. At that moment, all his fears about the procedure were confirmed, and he felt foolish for going along with it so complacently.

He felt that we should never do it again, whereas I felt fine and had no fears about continuing with the second treatment. If fainting was all that happened, it was a small price to pay to stop the miscarriages and bring my child into the world.

We went back to Nogales three weeks later for the second LIT treatment. Feeling more confident about the logistics, we flew in and out of Tuscon on the same day.

This time, we were much more blasé about the process. I was hoping I wouldn't pass out again, but if that did happen, at least we knew what to expect. In the three weeks since the first appointment, I scoured the internet and Yahoo message board for testimonials about the LIT experience and learned that strong reactions were more typical with the first treatment, but less likely with the subsequent ones.

As we waited for Eduardo at the same outdoor tables at McDonald's, we met a couple from Phoenix that was there for LIT as well. When Eduardo arrived, he greeted me like an old friend. In the minivan on the way to the office, I found myself acting as a guide, explaining the process to the other two couples that were new to LIT.

The process was exactly the same as the first time. The men had their blood drawn, and then we all went to the same Mexican restaurant for lunch. We came back to the office, and the women had their turn. The injections stung like last time, but I did not pass out. It was a non-event.

By now it was close to 2:00pm on a Saturday, so the border crossing was quite busy, but Dr. Sanchez and his staff had the process down. Eduardo went ahead of us to get in line at the border while we wrapped things up with the doctor, then the nurse walked us the two blocks to join him at the front of the border crossing line. We made it back to the Tucson airport with plenty of time to spare before our flight.

That night, as we crawled into bed, Nile turned to me and jokingly asked, "So what did you do today?"

"Oh, I flew to Mexico and back for a banned fertility treatment," I said, with a casual smirk. "Just a day in the life."

CHAPTER 30

After enduring two rounds of Lymphocyte Immunization Therapy, another blood test confirmed that it had achieved the desired result. My LADs were higher, which meant that my body was better prepared to protect an embryo. We were cleared to cycle.

We decided to try naturally at first. Maybe the LIT treatment, plus the medication cocktail prescribed by Dr. Peres, was all we needed to maintain a pregnancy. There was just one more step to complete my immune protocol.

Intravenous Immunoglobulin (or IVIG) is a blood product used to treat certain immune deficiencies. Dr. Peres prescribed a dose, calculated by weight, to be administered in the early part of my cycle so that my immune system would be balanced when the embryo, hopefully, implanted.

For me, IVIG seemed to have even more obstacles than LIT. Even though it was a legal pharmaceutical product, it was not covered by my insurance. One dose (thirty grams) plus the cost of the nurse to administer it was going to cost us about $3,000 out of pocket. If I could have been sure it was going to work and result in a baby, I wouldn't have hesitated. But I couldn't stomach paying a bill like that when the result was a big question mark.

Sometimes, in my late night research, I would come across someone donating or selling their unopened infertility medications. Once I realized that my IVIG cost about as much as cocaine, it made more sense. Many of them had paid only a copay for their IVIG drugs, so they were selling it for a lot cheaper than the pharmacy. There were a lot more risks in buying the drugs online, and I screened the sellers as best as I could. They also screened me, since they were practically giving away very valuable drugs. They wanted to be sure that I really needed the medicine and wasn't a scammer who was going to turn around and sell it for a profit.

Injections at all hours of the day, trips to Mexico, soliciting drugs online from strangers... if I hadn't felt like a junkie before, I sure did now.

During our holding pattern between the LIT treatments, Dr. Peres had called in the IVIG prescription to the specialized pharmacy. I tried every trick under the sun to get IVIG covered, but it wasn't going to happen. I'd read online about women who were successful with appealing the decision, but I didn't think I had the time or energy to waste. Going through the insurance appeals process could take months, during which time we would be racking up costs in other areas. Time was not on our side, to begin with. I was 35, which meant that all of my pregnancies from this point on would be considered high risk on account of my age.

So, I started procuring IVIG drugs from other fertility patients who no longer needed them. Once I had the drugs, I just needed a nurse to administer it.

Dr. Peres had put me in contact with an in-home nursing company that was contracted through the pharmacy to administer the drug. Once the prescription was called in, a nurse left a voicemail for me asking when I'd like to schedule my IV. When I called him back, I sort of felt him out. He seemed mellow. I told him that I actually procured the drugs outside of the pharmacy because I couldn't afford to buy them directly, and asked if he'd administer it for cash. He agreed without hesitation. I asked him how much he'd charge and he said, "Whatever you can do." He asked if I had all of the supplies for the IV. I didn't - all I had was the medication. He said he would bring the necessary supplies. I wondered how often he did this for patients like me, who got their drugs from alternate suppliers.

We set the appointment for the following week, after work. I had just started a full-time job at a new company. It takes three to four hours for the IVIG to empty into the bloodstream, so I mentally prepared myself to spend the evening on the couch. I prepared Nile, too, so that he would be home with me. I wanted him to be there in case I had some crazy reaction. Also, I didn't know this male nurse from Adam, so I'd feel safer if Nile was home.

When the nurse arrived, he seemed like a sweet man, not at all like he was going to kill me. He prepped everything and then reviewed the general procedure. He had to puncture me a few times to find a vein, but soon the IV was in and the meds were flowing. My only reaction was overall sleepiness, likely from the Benadryl I was instructed to take with IVIG. After four long hours, the treatment was over, and the nurse packed up his supplies. It was a relief to have another piece of the fertility puzzle in place. Still, it was a bit surreal for Nile and me to go about our regular bedtime ritual considering the abnormal day we'd just had.

We were at the crossroad of "Will this ever end?" and "I sure hope this works!"

During all the immunology intervention stuff, we had never stopped trying to get pregnant the old-fashioned way. I rejoined a Resolve support group to get, well, support. My new group was in a different part of town and included people that were mostly new to me. One of the reasons I wanted to go was to share my story. I hadn't had success yet, but I wanted to share what I'd learned about Reproductive Immunology. Since I had only learned about it from a friend in my previous Resolve group, I felt like it was my turn to share the information with someone else who might need it.

I talked about my suspicions of rejected embryos, and why it had motivated me to explore the RI field. I talked about all the hoops I had jumped through just to get a consultation, and the hurdles we had overcome before we were cleared to cycle.

I really wanted people to know that there were more ways to find answers than just repeating the pass/fail IVF process. My RI journey had revealed so much about what was going on in my body and offered practical treatment options that I wouldn't have known about otherwise. And all it had cost me was about $1,100 total. A failed IVF is over $15,000, and you are most often left with nothing. I'm an answers person, and although I still didn't have a baby, I had the next best thing – a scientific reason *why*.

After my story was finished, several women were intrigued and started asking me questions about the treatment. But, there were also people in the room giving off the this-girl-is-crazy vibe. The hostess of the group cut our discussion short. "This is all pseudoscience," she said dismissively.

Generally, other people's opinions don't matter to me, but this hurt. This was actually the most science anyone had ever applied to the case of my unexplained infertility and recurrent miscarriages. I felt I'd made a major breakthrough, and was compelled to share it with my tribe.

I was used to hurtful comments from people who were outside the infertility club and didn't know how to support me. But I couldn't believe that one of my own peers - a support group hostess, no less, who was committed to providing a safe place in which to tell my story - this woman straight up rejected me. After the meeting was over, I left and never went back.

What I realize now is that my story shined a light on something she did not want to see. And I understand that feeling. This was a road I didn't want to go down either when I had first heard about it. But I wasn't going to let reluctance stop me from searching for the cure to my health crisis. It takes courage and resilience to follow your curiosity, to keep putting your faith in one more person, one more solution, even after everything you've tried so far has failed.

I'm thankful that I was able to remain curious and open enough to recognize the cure when I finally found it.

CHAPTER 31

October, 2012

We relied solely on the immune treatment for several natural cycles. I was also seeing my acupuncturist regularly, taking all kinds of supplements and sticking to my AIP diet. After several months, when we still weren't pregnant, it was time to pull out all the stops. My next plan was to combine the full immune protocol with in vitro fertilization (IVF).

To be cleared to cycle again by Dr. Peres, I had to repeat the standard Reproductive Immunology blood work to determine the current state of my immune system. Once again, I had low LADs, which meant we were in for another round of LIT treatments in Mexico.

When Dr. Sanchez's assistant provided me with available LIT appointments, Nile pointed out that one of the dates coincided with his alma mater's football game against the

University of Arizona in Tucson. So we made a plan to take a morning LIT appointment, which would get us back to Tucson just as the game was getting underway. We would reward ourselves with football and margaritas for surviving another excursion to Nogales.

On the Saturday before Halloween, we flew to Tucson. The LIT appointment followed the same cadence as before - same process, same people, same reaction. It was all very textbook. After the treatment, we walked to meet Eduardo in the van at the border crossing. When we got to the front of the line, Eduardo collected our passports and handed them to the agent. The agent asked us the same question, to which we gave the same answer, "We are here for a medical procedure." I guess something seemed fishy to the agent because he pulled us over and ordered a full search of the van and our belongings. Another agent came over to "help," without even putting down his venti Starbucks Frappuccino. *There's a Starbucks around here?* I thought. *Is it proper that a border patrol agent is conducting official duties with one hand occupied by a beverage?*

I had about zero confidence in these folks, but I was at their mercy. They ordered us to leave all of our belongings (including our cell phones) in the car and to go inside. "Inside" was probably once a typical US government building, but the waiting room had been converted into a holding cell.

There were a few other people already locked inside when they added the five of us (Nile and I, one other couple, and Eduardo) to the room. I didn't want to talk too much or draw attention to myself since I was sure we were being watched, but I was also confident that I hadn't broken any laws. *What if our fellow fertility tourists have? What if the agents find something illegal in one of their bags? What if they hid something in one of MY bags?*

After about twenty minutes, an agent came to get us. He said the reason for the search was that they had found an apple in my husband's backpack during the cursory inspection, which required us to be removed from the car so that they could conduct a more extensive search. The apple was from the free breakfast at our hotel that morning. It had traveled from Tucson to Nogales and back, completely forgotten about in the bottom of his backpack. They threw the apple in the trash, and we all breathed easy, relieved to be getting on our way.

After Eduardo dropped us off at the McDonald's, we drove as fast as we legally could to Tucson and arrived on campus just as the game was starting. It was another beautiful day in the Arizona desert, and I was happy we were doing something fun. After the game, we went to a restaurant in the hills for Mexican food and margaritas. We encountered a lot of other people visiting from Los Angeles for the game, but had any of *them* tacked on a trip to Mexico to do something that was banned in the US? Probably more than I imagined.

A few weeks after LIT, we were cleared to cycle. I knew that there were no guarantees, but I was excited about starting the IVF process. In the past, there were a lot of stones I had wanted to turn over before we proceeded to IVF. Now, I felt that we had turned them all over. I was ready.

Dr. Silberman was confident and methodical about designing my drug protocol. At each ultrasound, we saw good follicle growth. My egg retrieval was scheduled for the day before Thanksgiving. The timing seemed fortuitous. We were very thankful to have eleven eggs retrieved, of which seven were mature and went on to fertilize. A few days later, the embryologist called to tell us that we were the proud parents of two beautiful embryos. A few days after Thanksgiving, we went in for the transfer. All went smoothly. I went home to rest for the day.

This time, Nile and I agreed not to do home pregnancy tests. We were concerned that it would cause too much mental stress. If it was positive, I'd be excited but instantly worried that something would go wrong. If it was negative (even a premature or false negative), I might go down some sort of devastated spiral.

Because the embryos were already five days old when they implanted, I only had to wait about ten days for the blood test to confirm my pregnancy instead of the usual fourteen days. Four days after the transfer, I woke up early due to a sharp cramp in my lower abdomen. I didn't know what to make of it, but I hoped it was implantation cramping. A few days later, I noticed that I was feeling fatigued and hungrier than usual.

On the day of the beta blood test, I woke up extra early so I could stop by the lab to have my blood drawn on my way to work. I was excited, but nervous. Today was the day. I wanted to know whether it worked, of course, but I almost wished that time could just stand still. *Can I just live in this moment of optimism before something comes along to crush it?*

From past experience, I wasn't expecting the call with the results until the afternoon. However, around 11:00 am, the nurse called to say that the blood test was positive. They wanted me to know at least that much right away and said they'd call later with the rest of the information.

Positive. Pregnant. Holy baby bump, it worked!

CHAPTER 32

November, 2012

I wish I could remember exactly how I told Nile that we were finally legitimately pregnant, but I can't. I imagine I called him at the office, rather than sending a text. But who knows. I do remember that we took a moment to absorb the news privately before I called my parents. Because the egg retrieval and embryo transfer procedures fell just before and after Thanksgiving, my parents knew that an IVF cycle was underway. They were visiting from out of state for the holiday, and I didn't want to keep it a secret. So now the news was out, but I asked everyone to keep it close to the chest until further notice.

After the initial beta, we had one or two follow-up betas, and the results of each were normal. Dr. Peres, the Reproductive Immunologist, monitored my immune system during the initial weeks of pregnancy and all was well. Our first ultrasound was scheduled at seven weeks gestation.

At this point, the fact that I was pregnant seemed a bit surreal. I'd made it farther than I'd ever made it before, with blood tests to prove it, but it just didn't seem real. I imagined that I would feel differently once I saw my little bean on the ultrasound monitor.

Nile took the morning off from work to go with me to our first ever ultrasound appointment. Just sitting in the waiting room, I felt like we'd crossed over some invisible barrier. We were no longer the ones scheduling fertility procedures and wondering when our ship would come in. Our hard work and dedication had paid off, we'd done it!

Dr. Silberman was on time as usual. He was happy and chatty with us. Even though he had had decades of experience with IVF, I could sense that it still put the wind in his sails to be able to tell a couple that they were expecting at long last. With this positive energy, he inserted the ultrasound wand and began to analyze what he saw on the screen. *I can't believe I'm about to see my baby.*

Then, complete silence.

It might have only been five seconds of silence, but it felt like a lifetime. Since we'd done dozens of ultrasounds with him before, I knew instantly that something was wrong.

He was the consummate professional, but his face spelled disappointment.

He explained to us that one, maybe both, embryos did indeed implant, but that all he could see was the sac. This wasn't a good sign. Sometimes, a fertilized egg will implant into the uterus but fail to develop into an embryo - a condition called "blighted ovum." He wanted us to come back in a few days for a second ultrasound to see if anything developed. He was kind and gentle, but matter-of-fact. It didn't look hopeful.

As he left the exam room, Nile and I sat in utter shock. Literally five minutes before, we were so excited to see our first baby for the first time. Now, there was no baby. Baby. No baby. Baby. No baby. I couldn't process this.

Moving in what felt like slow motion, I got dressed and prepared myself to face the world, my "expectant mom" label newly ripped off of me. I managed to make it through the lobby and the interminable wait for the dang elevator before I completely lost it outside the office building. Nile and I had driven separately so we could each go to work afterward. We stood on the sidewalk by my car, trying to make sense of everything. I think we went through all of the stages of grief in five minutes.

"What just happened? Weren't we just going in to see our baby and then he told us there is no baby?!" (Confusion, shock)

"Ok, let's go to work." (denial, avoidance)

"Are you kidding me?" (anger)

"I thought it actually worked this time." (embarrassment, frustration)

"Nope. My body is still failing me." (shame)

"What the f**k?" (numbness)

"If everything we did to get pregnant this time wasn't enough, what will ever be enough?" (reconstruction, reasoning)

We went round and round like this for a few minutes and then got into our cars, put on our seatbelts, and went to work. I somehow managed to hold it together at the office. But every spare minute at work and later at home, I went to Dr. Google searching for hope. *Has anyone been diagnosed with a blighted ovum at seven weeks gestation and then seen the baby at the next ultrasound?*

There wasn't much hope to be found on the internet. Or anywhere, really. I left the door cracked for the tiniest sliver of hope to shine in, but I understood where we were. I had an embryo (or two) implanted in my uterus that was strong enough to make me officially pregnant, but not complete enough to be viable. There's a unique kind of pain and grief for being pregnant with non-viable embryos.

When we returned to Dr. Silberman a few days later, I was resigned that this was going to end in miscarriage, and the ultrasound confirmed it. He suggested a dilation and curettage (D&C) to help speed the process along. He also suggested that it be performed by my OBGYN so that it would be covered by our insurance. I told him I didn't really have an OBGYN because I had separated from my last two, and it felt weird to include them now. Who knows how long I'd have to wait to schedule it. I didn't want to look someone up in the phone book to perform the D&C. He gently agreed to do it himself. We scheduled it for the last day in December.

Happy New Year.

CHAPTER 33

O n the morning of the D&C, Nile and I arrived at the clinic in the pre-dawn hours as instructed. We waited in the lobby for the nurse to call my name. When she did, she reminded us that men weren't permitted in the pre-op and recovery area, for the privacy of other female patients. However, since we were the only patients there at the moment, he was allowed to accompany me.

We were led back to the same exact pre-op/post-op space where I had waited to have my eggs retrieved about a month prior. Nile helped me out of my clothes and into a hospital gown. Then, he helped me settle into the hospital bed. We hardly said a word. There were no words for the awfulness of this day. How do you describe the despair of setting an alarm to get up before dawn on New Year's Eve to go have the "products of conception" scraped out of your uterus? My head was spinning from the emotional pain of walking the same halls where just a few days before we were excited about finally getting to see our baby for the first time. Now, we were completely drained of words and hope.

After a few minutes together in the pre-op area, the nurse came to escort Nile back to the waiting room because another female patient had arrived. I imagined the woman on the other side of the curtain, plump with ripe eggs to be retrieved for IVF. How hopeful she must be! How hopeful I'd been too.

Nile kissed me goodbye, and as he left, I started to quietly weep. I was alone with my pain in a room made of yellow surgical curtains and I wanted to die.

The nurse, Jennifer, came into my "room." She was warm and compassionate, like she instinctively knew how to handle me in this state. She didn't look at me with pity, but with knowing. She clearly understood my pain and had deep respect for what I was going through. While she prepped me for the procedure, I confided in her. I shared that we'd literally tried everything and still ended up here.

For the first time, I felt absolutely no hope. I'd turned over every rock, tried every combination there was to try. I'd done every crazy thing there is to do. I'd done Eastern medicine and Western medicine and everything in-between. I thought the immune meds plus IVF was a fool-proof plan. How could it not have worked? *Where do I go from here?*

She listened to me intently, pausing her work from time to time to look me in the eye and give me the extra empathy that I needed. She even cried a few tears with me. As she finished prepping me for the D&C, she said she knew someone that she thought could help me. "She's an acupuncturist, but she's more than that. She's a little woo-woo, but I believe she made the difference for me," she said, hinting at her own infertility struggles and subconsciously rubbing her new baby bump. From one southerner to another, I knew exactly what she meant by "woo-woo." Intuitive healers without their doctorates were referred to as "quacks" where we came from. But as West Coast transplants, we'd grown open-minded to fringe practices. Still, it's not for everyone.

Jennifer described a little bit of this woman's acupuncture practice and what she did to help her conceive. I really appreciated the referral, but if only I had a dime for every referral I'd been given to someone who got so-and-so pregnant. I had followed a lot of those leads and had nothing to show for it. *How is this one any different?*

As Jennifer wrapped up the pre-op preparations, she said she'd leave the acupuncturist's contact info for me with my discharge paperwork. Even in the hazy darkness of despair, the referral gave me the faintest flicker of hope.

That hope flickered for only a moment before Dr. Silberman came in, and my curiosity about the future was trampled by my abominable present. He was kind as he greeted me and went over the protocol. As he turned to head into the OR, he squeezed my foot like he was giving me a hug. Then the anesthesiologist came in, asked a couple of routine questions, and began the intravenous drugs that would render me oblivious. For one day, I didn't care how many pop stars it had killed, Propofol was my best friend.

"Count backward from 10," he said.

"10...9...8..." was all I could say before I was out.

I woke up alone in the same spot where I'd fallen asleep. Nurses popped in frequently to check on me and tell me that everything went well and that I could go home soon. When I was ready, the orderly would collect me and take me down to the car in a wheelchair. We'd done this whole wheelchair rigmarole a month earlier after the egg retrieval. That time, it seemed so unnecessary. I'd felt fine – buoyantly hopeful, actually. I didn't need the chair at all. But this time, I needed that wheelchair. Walking felt impossible. I needed someone to do what I couldn't.

Getting into the wheelchair, I felt weak and empty. The sadness dissipated and anger crept in. I just wanted to get the heck out of that place. The only thing this fertility clinic represented to me now was failure. *Expensive* failure.

I ruminated on my $15,000 miscarriage, looking for somewhere to assign the blame. *Was it the drug protocol? The doctor's fault? The embryologist's fault? Was this whole immune protocol a load of BS?* My mind fell deeper and deeper down the rabbit hole as the orderly pushed me through the glass doors into the fancy waiting room and I saw my husband's sad, sweet face looking up at me.

Together with the orderly, we headed for the elevator. Waiting for it to come, I sat crumpled in the wheelchair, tears running down my cheeks faster than I could wipe them away. I wanted to be strong, just long enough to get some privacy, but it just wasn't possible; I couldn't stop crying. While we waited, I didn't want to see anything or anyone, so I just looked down at my lap while continually wiping away tears with the sleeve of my sweatshirt. Another couple was hovering nearby, also waiting for the elevator. They were impeccably dressed and practically beaming - with hope or joy, I couldn't tell which. I could feel their quizzical gaze on me.

I felt ashamed. And exposed, which magnified the shame.
I was ashamed that I'd gotten my hopes up that this time
would work. I felt like I didn't belong. If ever there was the
opposite image of a fertile, pregnant woman, it is the image
of a woman who has just had two egg sacs scraped out of
her uterus, being pushed out of a fertility clinic in a wheelchair. Joining the mom club just wasn't in the cards for me.
I was a broken, barren, carved-out failure.

Minutes passed like hours, and it felt like the elevator would
never come. But finally, it did. As soon as the doors opened,
I felt a wave of relief that I could finally move away from the
clinic and toward home.

Once on the ground floor, the orderly wheeled me through
the lobby and out onto the busy street toward our car in the
parking lot. I wished for a secret tunnel that I could use to
escape in privacy instead of being wheeled down Wilshire
Boulevard with tears streaming down my face.

Back when I'd first heard about the clinic's special ameni-
ties reserved for celebrities and other wealthy clients, I just
thought it was par for the course in L.A. - a requirement for
doing business in Hollywood territory. In fact, I'd wondered
if the celebrities got better treatment; if maybe they were
the doctor's priority.

Now here I was, secretly wishing for my own bat-cave exit. It reminded me of the celebrity I had caught darting out of the back of a fertility clinic and into a waiting car. What if she was going through the same thing I was going through? In the aftermath of a D&C, being wheeled out of the clinic onto to a busy street – her grief would have been front-page news. *Nobody should have to go through that.*

This is what was going through my mind as I got into the car. *It could be worse. I could be hunted by the paparazzi in this state, feeling exposed, raw and wide open.* It was a surprise to myself that I could manage empathy at a time like this. Perhaps this was a signal that the worst of the emotional toll was behind me. Now, I just wanted to go home and move on with my life.

PART THREE:

The Rebuild

CHAPTER 34

My office was closed for the new year, which gave me two days to unplug and regroup. I needed it. Turned out, they didn't get everything during the D&C, so I still had to miscarry the old-fashioned way. Fun times.

I was grateful that I didn't have to deal with either going to work or calling in sick. I had some pain and cramping, but mostly I felt emotionally stripped. I felt very blah, overwhelmed, and tired. So tired. So blah.

Two days after the D&C, I thought it might make me feel better to sit outside and get some sun. It was one of those warm, sunny January days in LA that feels like a gift from the gods, even to someone in my mental state. Our condo complex had a sundeck and a pool. I only had to take a few steps. I could do that.

Hoping to expose my skin to the sun for some vitamin D, I ignored the chill and threw on a bikini. Seeing myself in the mirror, I was reminded of the weight I'd gained from IVF and the brief pregnancy. The comfy sweats I'd been wearing the past few days had hidden it from me. I found a wrinkled bathing suit cover-up in my closet and tried to banish negative thoughts about my body. I chose a chair by the pool and sat there with my eyes closed, completely motionless.

A voice startled me - "Hi!" I opened my eyes and saw a round-eyed girl about six years old looking at me through the iron gate that separated her building from mine. I'd never seen this kid before, but I gathered that she lived next door. As she started chatting at me, I thought, *get this kid out of here! Don't you know I just miscarried a baby? I can't deal with pesky kids right now!*

But the sweetness of the moment was stronger than the bitterness in my heart.

She told me about her teacher and favorite subjects in school, and a bunch of other topics I can't recall. I do remember that at some point she asked me if I had kids. "No, I don't," I said in a tone that would have subtly conveyed my disappointment to an adult, but it was understandably lost on her. I wondered if her mom knew where she was or if she was even allowed to be over here. But I was too exhausted to worry about her more than her own momma did, so I just laid back and let her talk my ear off through the fence for as long as she wanted. We had been talking for quite a while when, abruptly, she said she had to go and disappeared into her building.

As soon as she left, a little voice inside of me said that this little girl was sent to give me a message: *don't give up.* My own little girl was out there, waiting for me and trying to reach me. I would have years and years of conversations like this with my own child if I kept trying to bring her into this world.

For a moment, I couldn't believe I was really thinking this. *Have I gone totally crazy? Has the West Coast woo-woo finally rubbed off on me?*

But it felt real to me at that moment. I wasn't going to tell anyone else that I had met a child outside of my apartment building that had been sent to me (by who? the universe? God?) to deliver a message from my unborn, not even conceived child. Nope, I was going to keep this to myself.

I wrapped the encounter with the little girl around me like a blanket. My soul needed warming, and I would take it wherever I could get it.

The truth is that, even before our infertility journey, I had been on the woo-woo path. My teachers were Oprah, Martha

Beck, Eckhart Tolle, Louise Hay, Wayne Dyer, Caroline Myss, and Pema Chodron, to name a few. Through their writings, I slowly unlearned destructive thoughts and behaviors. My eyes were opened to new ways of thinking.

I learned that this was the typical pattern that I followed - seek out healing, feel better, then forget most of what I learned and go back to my old ways. I would climb to the peak of emotional health, forget to maintain it, spiral, then start the climb all over again. I knew that if I let my mind run free now, I would get sucked down another victim-shame spiral.

After the little girl disappeared, I stayed outside, enjoying the weather and allowing my bitterness to thaw. My conversation with Nurse Jennifer came to mind. Who was this new acupuncturist? I wanted to trust the referral, but in LA it's easy to find people who claim to have the magic cure-all. But something about that moment with Jennifer seemed holy. Important.

I thought about it a little while and decided I had nothing to lose. The little girl on the other side of the fence had tilted the scales for me that day – toward optimism. I was sure we were done with fertility treatments for a while, perhaps working with someone in the interim would help me feel like I was doing *something*.

From my chair on the sun deck, I sent an email to the acupuncturist's office. I wasn't going to spiral again. I was determined to heal.

CHAPTER 35

After the New Year holiday that I spent recovering from my D&C, I went back to work and tried to carry on with my life. Nile had previously planned a trip to visit his family, and I told him it was fine to go ahead and go. I'd spend the week taking care of me. I'd be fine.

Turns out, I wasn't fine. I was majorly depressed and hormonally screwed up. I was shuffling through my daily life, pretending to care.

All I did was go to work and come home. I was glad to have the distraction, but it wasn't enough. And, since it was January, it was dark when I left for the office and dark when I came home. It felt like my day was over just as I was free. Wake up, go to work, come home, go to bed. My world was very small and without joy.

The first night Nile was gone, I ordered a gluten-free pizza (something I hadn't allowed myself to eat for several months because I had been avoiding dairy and tomatoes) and ate it while I watched reality TV. I thought relaxing my diet and vegging out would make me feel better, but it made me feel more alone and unhealthy. I snuggled with Clancy and tried to ride it out.

The second night, I came home from work and reheated a slice of pizza, settling into my couch. Unable to get my mind off the miscarriage, I began thinking crazy thoughts and went down a rabbit hole of depression, confusion, and hopelessness. I convinced myself we'd never have a child, that my body just wasn't going to do this. But I still couldn't imagine my life without children.

Really, what I couldn't imagine was failure. I couldn't even look at the fact that this might not work out for us. Failure was not an option. But I felt like I'd done all that I could possibly do. If the immune protocol paired with IVF didn't work, what on earth would? Possibly nothing. I wanted a child in my life, and a life without one might not be worth living.

I wasn't sure I could get out of the hole. In fact, I knew I couldn't - not by myself, anyway. I needed to talk to someone or I was going to go out of my mind. The next Resolve group meeting was over a week away, which felt like the distant future. I knew I needed professional help, but that wasn't going to materialize soon enough either. Almost none of my friends knew we had done IVF or that we'd miscarried. I'd been keeping it all pretty close to the chest. The thought of calling up an unsuspecting friend and laying all this on her felt like too heavy a burden, for both of us. Luckily there was one person I knew I could call, my friend Alexis.

Alexis was a childhood friend who, as fate would have it, was living in Los Angeles when Nile and I arrived. The move to LA was very overwhelming for me – the sprawl, the traffic, the density, the starting over – she was an anchor for me during that time. Our apartments were some distance apart, but I visited her just about every other weekend until she moved away. She was a little slice of home, of the old me, in this concrete-but-seventy-two-degrees-and-sunny jungle.

Alexis was now a busy working mom who had had her own complicated, heartbreaking fertility journey. She had experienced traumatic miscarriages and gone through at least one D&C before carrying a successful pregnancy to term. She was a safe person to talk to, with the experience to say something helpful.

Alexis quickly replied to my SOS text and called me as soon as she had put her kids to bed. I unleashed all of my "crazy" on her, things like "What if the babies were perfectly fine but they couldn't see them well enough on the ultrasound and they just scraped out the only children I was ever going to have? What if they killed my children?!" Hearing myself say it out loud, it made me cringe. *I have totally lost my mind.*

After two seconds of silence, Alexis replied, "Oh my gosh, I thought the same thing. I literally thought my doctor was purposely killing my babies." And just like that, I was validated. I wasn't crazy, and I wasn't alone anymore.

We went on to talk about other crazy thoughts, and she shared how she got through those hard days. Only a couple of years earlier, Alexis had been in this same dark place, and she had gone on to recover and have twins. I wasn't sure how to get from point A to point Z, but through her example, I could see that it was possible.

At that moment, my spiral ended.

During my final weekend alone, I put together a wellness "staycation" to keep myself on a good path. I didn't normally indulge in so much self-care, but it seemed essential right now. I'd rather be alive and a couple hundred dollars poorer than the inverse.

On Saturday, I had a wonderful massage and soak at a local day spa. On the way home, I stopped by our local juicery to place an order for a one-day juice fast that I would pick up and drink the next day. I was bloated from IVF, and a general detox sounded good to me. I'd never been one to fast, in fact it intimidated me, but looking at all those bottles of colorful juice in the refrigerator, I didn't see how it could hurt. *I can always eat some food if I get too hungry right? No one is keeping score.*

On Sunday morning, I threw on a sweatshirt over my pajamas and took the dog outside to do his business. Then I hustled over to the juice bar to pick up my sustenance for the day: $50 worth of fresh juice, which seemed like nothing after a $15,000 miscarriage. I drank my juice. I called my mom. I cleaned my house. Then, I went on a long walk on the beach with Clancy to get my blood pumping and clear my mind.

As we walked, I began to see that it wasn't enough to take control in the doctor's office. If I was going to survive this, I needed to take control at home, too. I had learned to assert myself in my relationships with medical professionals, now I was learning to assert myself over my own weaknesses. To reach out when I was alone with my demons, and call for back-up if they were winning. To make healthy choices even when no one was looking, even when I wasn't actively trying to conceive.

At the end of the weekend, I felt rejuvenated and had the clarity that I would survive this. I welcomed Nile home with a smile, confident that I had turned a corner.

CHAPTER 36

Ten days after my conversation with the little girl through the fence, I was in the car on the way to my first appointment with the new "woo-woo" acupuncturist. Her name was Danica. I thought about how effortlessly all the pieces had fallen into place to allow this to happen. A referral from a caregiver, Danica's instant reply to my email, the realization that she was just a mile or so away from my house and had Saturday appointments open...everything about it felt right.

I was really curious about how her acupuncture practice differed from the three I'd gone to before. What made it so special? I was excited, but still wracked by pessimism. All I seemed to be able to do was miscarry.

The office was cozy. I sunk into a comfy couch and looked around at the wall art displaying positive affirmations and fertility language. Soon, Danica came in to greet me and showed me to a treatment room that was softly lit by a dimmed lamp in the corner.

She asked what brought me to her office that day, and through a torrent of tears, I told her everything I thought was relevant from the last few years. She knew a lot about fertility treatments and Reproductive Immunology, so she asked dozens of questions and took a ton of notes.

We talked for almost an hour. It felt so good to be able to lay my story on someone who wasn't a friend or family member. In the back of my mind, I kept thinking that surely any minute she would abruptly end the conversation and ask me to lie down for the needles. But, she didn't. She seemed to have all the time in the world. It was very validating, I immediately felt that she was completely dedicated to helping me.

When she asked me to lie down on the table for the needles, I was ready. We'd gone over so much of my traumatic history, I needed a rest. After the needles were in and she left the room, I fell quickly asleep.

She let me sleep a long time, knowing I needed as much rest as possible. She came into my room just as I woke up naturally. Like she intuitively knew when it was time. My last infertility acupuncturist had used a timer, which gave me such anxiety because I felt pressured to hurry up and fall asleep before the timer went off.

With Danica, I could let it all go and trust that she would take care of me. She entered the room calmly and quietly, asking how I was feeling. I was in such a post-nap haze that all I could utter was, "better." I felt like I'd slept for a decade. I wondered how long I'd been in here and if Nile was worried about me, having been gone so long. She quickly removed all the needles and told me to take my time getting off the table and getting dressed.

I shuffled out into the lobby area to check out and schedule my next appointment. On the counter, Danica placed two bottles of Chinese herbs. She'd written on the top of each bottle cap how many to take each day. I was relieved to see the herbs she prescribed were in pill form. I had come to dread the horrible teas that my previous acupuncturists prescribed, drinking them made me feel like I was punishing myself every day. *Had that daily negative reinforcement hurt my chances of conceiving?*

As she described the herb protocol, she paused and said, "Sometimes I take one pill once a day, and other times I take four pills twice a day. I just open the bottle and shake a few out. However many come out is what I take." I gave her a look. *What are you telling me? Am I supposed to take the pills as prescribed, or am I supposed to take what magically pops out of the bottle?* In response to my non-verbal query, she smiled and said, "Just know that I do that sometimes."

As we wrapped up our epic three-hour appointment, she mentioned a special fertility workshop that she was hosting the next day and asked if I was interested in attending. It was a mind-body spiritual and nutritional program she'd created for women experiencing infertility. She explained that the program provided a good foundation for understanding the way she practiced fertility acupuncture and would help me get more out of our time together. It felt like we were moving too fast. *I just paid almost $400 for acupuncture and herbs, and now she's asking me to write a check for another couple hundred for a workshop tomorrow?*

It was too much for me to process in my post-acupuncture haze, but I felt that I could trust her. She wasn't trying to upsell me, she really thought that I could benefit from the program. My instincts said that she was walking this path with me, and I chose to follow her lead.

When I arrived home later than planned on that Saturday afternoon in January, I tried to explain to Nile what we did in the session. "She talked to me for a long time," I stammered. "She gets it. It was very relaxing." I was having a hard time putting my experience into words. Even though I had turned a corner, Nile could sense my daily struggle to keep healing. I was making steady progress, but there were still days that I lost the battle. He didn't exactly understand what I was trying to say about my first experience with Danica, but he understood that she made me feel better. At the time, that was all that mattered.

CHAPTER 37

It just so happened that Danica's workshop was hosted at my fertility clinic. It felt like returning to the scene of a crime. But maybe there was a reason that I was supposed to return. I was definitely still wounded, but I was brave enough to go. Even though I was still a little depressed and cynical, I wasn't going to give up.

During her three-hour workshop, Danica introduced us to the concept of eating right for particular phases of our cycle. She explained why certain foods were good for certain times of the month and gave us shopping lists and recipes. She even brought some dishes and homemade soups for us to sample.

She also addressed the emotional and spiritual components of fertility. Many of us had had doors slammed in our faces, been called crazy, told we needed to just have more sex, and so on. We had had many obstacles to overcome, and we were often doing it alone. I had seriously considered counseling, but I never felt that a therapist was the right person to help me through this journey because it would take me months just to catch them up on the back story. I didn't want help processing my losses, I wanted help moving forward and resolving my infertility. However, it made me realize that I certainly needed to talk to a professional. After that workshop, I started to understand the magic of Danica's practice.

I expected her to be skilled with needles, Chinese herbs, and women's health issues. What impressed me most was that she also had in-depth knowledge about infertility treatments, local doctors and even the autoimmune component of infertility. She understood my language, my story, and my path. She didn't second-guess decisions I'd made. In the past, my acupuncturists were undoubtedly well-meaning, but there was a limit to their knowledge on these topics. I often got the message from them that I could find success with acupuncture alone. By then I knew that this was bigger than acupuncture, and was relieved that Danica didn't seem to be pushing it as a sole solution.

In the early appointments, we didn't visit the subject of fertility treatments and what my next steps would be. I wasn't ready. My body was not healed yet. My period had not returned, and I was dealing with another physical side of effect from the D&C: my hair was falling out.

Gobs and gobs of hair fell out every day. At first, I thought, "Okay, I can deal with this for a few days." Days turned into weeks, and before I knew it, more than half of my hair was gone.

I scoured the internet looking for answers, reading every anecdote and testimonial I could dig up. I kept finding stories of women who lost a lot of hair after having a baby, but hardly any stories of hair loss after a miscarriage or D&C. Was I all alone here? I couldn't help but think, *If I had a baby in my arms and lost all my hair I would be okay with that. No hair and no baby is just too much to take.*

My anxiety about losing my hair was not a crisis of vanity; it was about my loss of privacy. Just as I was starting to turn the corner on my mental health, my hair abandons me. It broke my heart each time I took a shower and found skeins of hair clinging to my wet hands.

I cried in the shower more during those hair loss days than after any of my miscarriages. *When will it stop? What if I go completely bald?*

Every day, I woke up hoping that the shedding had stopped and I could move on from this post-miscarriage hell. I researched good shampoos for hair loss and ran out to the health food store on my lunch break to procure them. Again,

I found myself holding these bottles in the check-out line wondering, *hoping* that I was holding the cure in my hands. Each day, I pulled my hair into a ponytail or bun, trying to make my thinning hair less noticeable. But, no matter how I styled my hair for work, strands would fall down onto my desk every time I leaned over to scrutinize a printed report. I would be lost in the flow of work, completely forgetting about my pain for a sweet moment, when a discarded hair would interrupt the peace to remind me of everything.

I felt humiliated for trying to go on with life, especially at work. By the time it ended, I'd lost at least two-thirds of my hair. A passing stranger at Target may not notice, but my coworkers sure did.

I was drowning. But at every Saturday appointment, I could count on Danica to throw me a life preserver. It is not an exaggeration to say that she saved me. By midweek, I was counting down the days until our next appointment, knowing my sanity was always saved on Saturday.

After a couple of months, I felt a strong pull to get out of town and see something new. It was more than a whim, this seemed urgent. I needed to feel more alive. President's Day weekend was coming, so I planned a two-night stay for Nile and me just a few hours away in the wine country of Paso

Robles. We would drive up the coast right after my Saturday morning appointment with Danica.

As we wound our way north into nature, I felt my body relax. We checked into our hotel and settled into our room, where I popped my second daily dose of Chinese herbs, and another wave of relaxation came over me. We located a nearby wine bar where we could kill time before dinner. That weekend, there was no such thing as too much wine.

As we bellied up to the bar, Nile received an email from his boss that could only be described as a tirade. His boss aggressively chastised Nile for going out of town, explaining that he needed "all hands on deck," even on a Saturday night. Nile had no idea where this was coming from because he was up-to-date on all of his projects, or so he thought. This was a relatively new job for Nile, so this sudden disapproval from his new boss was cause for panic. Our brief respite from the stress of work and health issues was dashed.

We finished our wine and crossed the street for dinner, the whole time discussing Nile's boss and what his email really meant. Frustrated that work stress was following us, we hardly enjoyed our dinner under the stars. *Can't we go out on a Saturday night in peace?*

As we opened the door to our hotel room, I saw something on the table that hadn't been there when we left - a plate of cheese and crackers covered with plastic wrap. The note taped to the top listed our last name and room number. *Oh, that's nice of the hotel to send*, I thought. But I didn't remember reading anything about a complimentary in-room snack. I didn't eat cheese or crackers, but still. Then, I noticed a typed note inside the folded-over piece of paper with our name and room number. I open it, wondering who it could possibly be from, since to my knowledge nobody knew where we were staying. As soon as I read it, I dropped the paper like it was on fire.

The note said, "Love, your daughter." Was this some kind of practical joke? Here we were, recovering from a miscarriage, and someone sent us a cheese plate with a note from "our daughter"? *Sorry, you must have the wrong room. All we have is nonviable embryos and pregnancies that end too soon. No daughter, thank you very much!*

I showed the note to Nile and asked him if he had told anyone about our getaway. He was just as confused as I was - nobody knew where we were staying. I called the front desk and the young man who answered said that the notes were all in their system - someone had sent us the cheese plate, but there was no record of who. "But I don't have a daughter," I said. "Hmm," said front desk guy. "Well, please enjoy the cheese and crackers anyway, they were definitely for you." *Ummm...okay.*

By now, I was officially onboard the woo-woo train, with my Chinese herbs on the bedside table, my mind open to signs and spiritual gifts, but this... *THIS*... was taking it too far. I could not believe I'd received a literal message - on a cheese plate no less - that said, "Love, your daughter."

Did this really just happen?

CHAPTER 38

Back in La La Land, Nile and I resumed our regular work schedules and tried not to be creeped out by our disappointing weekend away in Paso Robles. It turned out that the issue with Nile's boss was a big misunderstanding. Nile shared with him the reason for our trip, and his boss felt so bad that he and his wife wanted to take us to dinner to make up for the drama he had caused. *Oh great. Now, Nile's boss and colleagues know about our infertility woes too.* Regardless of my feelings, I figured we had to accept their offer to keep the peace.

As the weeks and months progressed, I continued to work hard during the week and to see Danica on Saturdays. My hair finally stopped falling out. One morning, as I gingerly combed and styled the hair I had left, I noticed lots of new hairs popping up. "All is not lost," I quipped. As I healed, my attention slowly shifted from the past to the present. I focused on my overall wellness by eating healthy foods and going to yoga, in addition to my weekly acupuncture sessions. I tried to get out in the sun as often as I could, even if only for a few minutes on my lunch break. I had a new boss at work, so I kicked into high gear and developed aggressive plans for the projects that I ran. I hired critical members of my team, and soon we were a well-oiled machine. I felt like I was back!

In a silo, my job was great. I was well equipped to do the work, and the level of responsibility was fully aligned with my capabilities. After many years of being underemployed, this felt good! My new boss seemed to be noticing my abilities and even shared the big plans he had for me. But all was not well.

I found myself butting heads with some of my peers, as well as the owner of the company. The repetitive battling, the constant obsessing, wore on me. My awesome team provided a safe place for me, and my new boss seemed like an ally too. But, I had a hard time reconciling the two realities of my job; it was the best job I'd ever had, but it was also the most destructive and volatile.

My personal drama had loomed so large that it eclipsed everything else, and until then I had failed to see how detrimental my work life had become. I'd had pretty serious work drama for the whole of my fifteen-year career, this just seemed par for the course. I attributed my situation to the career path I'd chosen, and if I couldn't change my career then I would do my best to work around it. I thought I was doing a good job of practicing self-care, but Danica sensed my inner battles. I had more work to do.

After the initial triage phase of rebuilding my mind, body, and spirit back to a functional level, she started giving me homework assignments. They were mostly writing assignments, challenging me to turn inward and explore the unopened boxes of my inner conflict.

In response to one such assignment, this is what I wrote:

(Danica's Prompt: Breaking up with infertility)

F**k you, infertility. I am so over you. You have ruled my life for too long, and I am OVER it. I'm done. We're through.

I surrender. You win. I've fought the good fight, and now I am done fighting. Bravo! To the victor go the spoils. I'm taking off my warrior princess crown and retiring it forever. I am not fighting with you anymore.

I am not fighting with A----

I am not fighting with M----

I am not fighting with K----

... or anyone else from work

My baby girl is trying to show me that I still have work to do in this area - work relationships. I can't be waging these unnecessary battles anymore. This is causing my autoimmune disease. I need to follow the current, the flow that my baby is trying to teach me.

I need to understand that my best is enough. If there is anyone in my life that does not think my best is enough, then they are cut.

It's not about being perfect, it's about being my best. Fighting with people from work is about me being right and them being wrong. That is not the way. 'The way' is doing *my* best, and recognizing when they are doing *their* best. If I want people to accept my best, I have to accept the best that other people offer as well.

Phew...ok. I got the lesson."

CHAPTER 39

In addition to the physical benefits of Danica's acupuncture treatments, I was lucky to have someone else to talk to besides Nile. I had wonderful friends, but I was so deep in the hole that their support barely scratched the surface. I continued to see Danica every week. Slowly but surely, after four months of weekly treatment, my body healed and my hair was growing in thicker. She thought I was ready to try to get pregnant again.

As before, we decided to try naturally for a few months before putting our chips on a fertility intervention. During one visit, Danica thought she felt a pregnant pulse. I was giddy with excitement! I suspected that I was pregnant too – I had noticed the signs. But by our next session, I'd gotten my period. It was all too familiar.

She asked me how I felt about going back to Dr. Silberman. I was on the fence. I felt like I'd gone as far as I could go with him, but he was "the best" so who else could I go to?

Danica suggested that I have a consult with a different doctor, Dr. Rollins. She said that Dr. Rollins would approach my case like a detective. She also mentioned that she had a direct line of communication with Dr. Rollins, they could work on my case as a team.

I thought about her advice for a while. I definitely needed a detective! I needed someone to realize that my case wasn't ordinary, someone who wouldn't just put me through the paces that they put everyone else through. I was still pretty jaded toward reproductive endocrinologists and the whole infertility process, but someone I trusted was telling me to consider something. I decided to listen, and scheduled a consultation with Dr. Rollins.

I'd met Dr. Rollins once before, she had filled in for Dr. Silberman while he was out of town. She was young and serious, but kind. During our consult, she reviewed my records and asked me a few questions. There were several big realms she wanted to scrutinize further: thyroid, genetic abnormalities, autoimmune issues, infectious disease, and anatomical issues. I could see the detective side working as she explained her approach.

Almost every doctor I'd ever seen told me my thyroid was normal, but Dr. Rollins thought my thyroid stimulating hormone (TSH) was a little too high for optimal pregnancy. Dr.

Peres, the Reproductive Immunologist, had also prescribed medication for my thyroid, so they were on the same page. I'd gone off all the immune meds after the D&C, but I was still on the thyroid meds. Dr. Rollins said to keep taking it.

When I asked her what she thought of the immune protocol that Dr. Peres had prescribed, she was clearly uncomfortable with it. She didn't see the need for LIT, IVIG, and the rest of it. She said that studies had not consistently shown any benefit. I expected this response but was a little disappointed that she didn't agree.

Since I was getting (but not staying) pregnant on occasion and had no known anatomical issues, she thought we should try IUI again. It seemed crazy to do an eighth IUI, but I couldn't argue with her logic, and I liked that she didn't jump straight to IVF. She ordered a few blood tests that no one had ordered before. She also prescribed a round of antibiotics to clear any latent infections before the next cycle.

Her thoroughness gave me a good feeling. Working with her felt more "right" to me than working with Dr. Silberman. I was willing to try it her way. I knew I couldn't do this alone, and my intuition told me that Dr. Rollins was the right ally. And she was.

I went to the lab and had my blood drawn for the new tests.

CHAPTER 40

May, 2013

U p to this point, my journey had been split between two "modes" - trying to get pregnant naturally, and trying to get pregnant with medical intervention. It was a carousel that I had been riding in circles for five years now: Google stuff, self-diagnose, try naturally, give up, see a doctor, expensive failed interventions, regroup, Google stuff, self-diagnose, and on and on.

Yet, something at this point in the journey gave me the strength to continue, but not in a circle. This time, instead of working toward pregnancy, I was working toward health. Health for *all* of my body, not just my baby-making parts. Health for the sake of *being healthy*, not just getting pregnant.

For example, right around this time I bit the bullet and had some long-overdo dental work done. I had an ill-fitting crown on my molar that had been bugging me for a decade;

but in the midst of IVF and shots and acupuncture and gut problems, an irritated spot on my gums didn't even register. Now, I decided to get it fixed.

I also spent some time enjoying life with my husband. Hadn't we been a happy family of two before all of this? Previously, I'd been too depressed and out of sorts to plan a trip. But after I turned the corner on my recovery, the time was right. Nile and I jetted off to Hawaii for a week of rest and relaxation. Life was still good, and I could still live it even if I couldn't control it. We had a great time, and I returned feeling better than ever. My cup was full.

After our vacation, I got the results of the blood tests Dr. Rollins had ordered. It turned out my anti-mullerian hormone level (AMH) was really low. AMH gauges "ovarian reserve," the number of eggs a woman has left. It looked like I didn't have very many. But at 36, I was still relatively young, and Dr. Rollins didn't want to base all of our decisions solely on the results of one test. She said it was just a bit more information about what was going on in my body. One more piece of the puzzle.

Another thing she tested me for was a genetic marker called Fragile X - a syndrome linked to intellectual disabilities and autism. Doctors sometimes request this screening when a woman has a hard time conceiving or has potential premature ovarian insufficiency. I didn't have the mutation, but I was in the "gray zone." This basically meant that there wasn't much danger of our children being affected, but Dr. Rollins explained that if I were to have a daughter, she would be wise to freeze her eggs early on. I made a mental note for my future daughter. *Freeze your eggs, and thanks for the cheese plate.*

The big "ah-ha!" moment hit when Dr. Rollins discovered that my estrogen was low in the luteal phase (the period of time between ovulation and the onset of menstruation). It's important to have enough estrogen during that phase so that the egg follicles develop optimally. Too little estrogen and they won't be viable. When hormone levels aren't optimal, the eggs that result during the cycle aren't "strong enough," which throws off the cycle and endangers the pregnancy.

I understood that low estrogen in the luteal phase was most likely causing my premenstrual spotting. From the very beginning of this journey, spotting had been my first signal that something was off. How could a baby implant in my uterus with all these cells sloughing off? Now, five years and more than a dozen miscarriages later, this doctor had essentially validated my original hypothesis.

I had read that acupuncture could stop spotting. By that point, I had seen four different acupuncturists over the course of five years, and none of them had been able to stop it. In the Tao of Fertility by Dr. Daoshing Ni* he states that the cause of premenstrual spotting is that the egg is too weak. While many doctors treat spotting in the luteal phase by adding progesterone, the root of the issue - as I now understood it - is that the egg isn't strong enough to begin with, so the corpus luteum (left behind after the egg pops out) doesn't produce enough progesterone. When not enough progesterone is present, the cells begin sloughing off prematurely, which results in spotting. A progesterone supplement in the luteal phase can stop the spotting, but it only treats the symptom, not the cause, and actually makes the problem worse.

Dr. Rollins said the treatment for low estrogen in the luteal phase was to take an oral estrogen supplement during the week before my period. This would help the eggs that we recruited for the next cycle to have the best start.

Now we were treating the cause, not the symptom. This was huge.

It was incredible to me that I'd been asking OBGYNs and fertility doctors about my spotting for almost a decade and no one had bothered to run this simple estrogen test until now. The treatment was a $10 prescription. A week of pills for $10. We'd spent almost $100,000 on fertility treatments, not to mention the lost pay from jobs I had left to pursue starting a family. And now, a $10 prescription might be the solution. Holy cow.

We agreed that our next step would be an IUI with a combination of Clomid and injectable medicines to increase the number of eggs we had to work with. I would take the estrogen the week before my period and then come in to start the IUI cycle once my period began. This is referred to as estrogen priming protocol (EPP). Doctor Rollins was convinced that I didn't need the autoimmune drugs and wanted me to stop taking them. I was reluctant, but I decided to trust her and do things her way.

This IUI cycle, my eighth, was relatively uneventful. By the third day of Clomid, I had a horrible headache again. Since I only had to take it for five days, I just dealt with it. The ultrasounds showed decent follicle growth – it looked like we'd have three or four eggs. The IUI procedure went off without a hitch, and we went on with our lives while we waited to find out if it had worked.

About a week after our IUI, I started to notice pregnancy symptoms. I had on-and-off breast pain and twinges and pressure in my uterus. I started taking a home pregnancy test every other day. The first one was positive. Honestly, at this point, I didn't need a pregnancy test to tell me what I already knew. But I had learned that doctors take you way more seriously if you say you have a positive pregnancy test than if you say, "I feel like I'm pregnant."

I took a second test two days later. It was positive - and it was darker! But the next evening, my right hip started to ache. I had jabbing pain in my right ribs and straining on the right side of my neck. The next pregnancy test was still positive - but the line was lighter. This wasn't good.

CHAPTER 41

I emailed Dr. Rollins to update her on my positive pregnancy tests and the symptoms I was experiencing - first of pregnancy, then pregnancy loss. It was hard to balance my enormous respect for her with the heartbreak of another possible miscarriage. The frustration was indescribable. I'd miscarried while trying naturally, IVF and multiple IUIs. How many doctors did it take to help me miscarry? Why was I spending so much money to achieve the same result as when we got pregnant naturally?

Still, I asked for a blood test to confirm my chemical pregnancy. The test showed that I was pregnant, but - as I suspected - it wasn't viable. Going forward, Dr. Rollins wanted me to be on a steroid to calm my immune system. She was finally addressing my immune system issues; apparently all I had to do to convince her was miscarry again.

This miscarriage was harder on me physically than any chemical pregnancy I'd experienced before. I woke up in the middle of the night in agony and shook Nile awake, begging him to get me some Advil. For several days afterward, I was emotionally and hormonally drained. Maybe I hadn't escaped the carousel after all. Maybe this would only end when I accepted defeat. I felt out of it.

My friend Reba was visiting from New York, and I was faced again with the unique agony of wanting to confide in someone, but knowing that their attempts to help would probably make the pain worse. I had once shared with her how I had found the Resolve support group to be very helpful. As a mental health therapist, I asked if she'd heard of the organization. Her reply was, "No. My clients are dealing with much more serious problems." Ouch. I loved Reba like a sister and immediately forgave her in my heart. But after that, I avoided the topic of my miscarriages when we were together.

Nevertheless, I welcomed the distraction of enjoying a weekend with her. While we browsed vintage stores on Melrose, ate organic ice cream and sunned ourselves under the palm trees overlooking the Pacific Ocean, I couldn't help but wonder...*where do I go from here? Maybe it just isn't going to happen. Life is pretty good. Am I making it harder by fighting this battle?*

Nile and I went back to trying naturally, and I continued to see Danica weekly. By this point, we were mostly working on the spiritual and emotional components of fertility. One of the exercises she asked me to do was to visualize a life without kids. The thing that I feared most was that I would fail in my mission to bring children into the world - that time, money and all other resources would run out before I solved the puzzle. Since this was something I feared, Danica wanted me to explore it. Not necessarily to accept it, but to *imagine* accepting it.

What would our life be like without kids? I had never truly considered it. So, I sat down and wrote a list of how I visualized our life together, just Nile and me. We'd travel, eat great food and have nice furniture. I'd be an awesome aunt to my three nephews. We'd have a good life.

This version of my future felt sad because I knew we would make good parents and the world would be better off with our kids in it. But the exercise helped me to see, if only barely, that life would still be okay if we didn't have children. We'd have more money and be well rested. *The world will not end if I don't have a baby. The Pacific Ocean will still be blue, the sun will still rise and set, and I can either be against it or at peace with it.*

I started to skip the occasional Saturday appointment with Danica. For the last nine months or so, I'd surrendered. I hadn't pushed for infertility treatments or other road-less-traveled interventions. I simply showed up on Saturdays, dedicated to feeling human again.

I'd gotten so much out of my time with Danica for the last nine months. She had pulled me out of the quicksand after my traumatic miscarriage, and I would forever be in her debt for that alone. My body had bounced back to the point that I'd been pregnant twice more under her care. It was miraculous to observe.

However, I was still miscarrying. Her wisdom alone was not enough to get me all the way to the finish line. If we were going to keep at it, we were going to need the whole team on board.

I wasn't willing to miscarry anymore.

CHAPTER 42

Trying on the what-if-we-never-have-kids mindset felt like standing at a fork in the road. One weekend, I headed to Texas to visit my family before going on to Chicago for a work conference. While hanging out with my nephews at my parent's house, enveloped by the sweet chaos that can only be called "three boys under five years old," I contemplated my role in the family. Was I the jet-setting child-free aunt, popping in from time to time to dip my toes into the world of raising children? Or, would I someday be a mom myself - a master of the chaos?

Sitting on my parent's couch, clutching a cup of coffee as toys whizzed across the room, I could see the benefit of not having children. The house would be cleaner. Our couch would be free of milk stains. We could have nice things. There wouldn't be any pee on the floor by the toilet from toddler misfires. Parenting suddenly seemed very messy. *How dirty am I willing to get?*

I could see what the lesson from my last exercise with Danica was teaching me. I could sit there on that couch and wish that I had children of my own, ruining my stuff and playing with their cousins, while simultaneously enjoying the freedom of my kid-free life.

It was a big "let go" moment for me. I could clearly see my life going in either direction. Maybe my death-grip on solving the puzzle had caused the answer to elude me. Maybe I needed to step back and accept what my life *was* instead of obsessing over what I wanted it to be.

I still preferred the version of my future where I had kids. I was pretty sure that if I did nothing, I would never have a baby. So, having a baby meant that I would have to continue the fight. *Do I have anything left in the tank?*

As I sat there, having my revelation, I watched my parents interact with their grandsons. They are amazing grand-parents, each in their own way. My mother is extremely giving. She will go to the ends of the earth to create one more moment of joy for her grandchildren. No holiday or occasion goes uncelebrated in her house. My father leads by example and enjoys teaching his grandsons to hit a base-ball or chop vegetables for a salad. They both show up to all the important events in their grandkids lives. I couldn't help but think how lucky these boys were to have grand-parents like them.

I enjoyed witnessing the family dynamics during my visits home, but something was missing: my children. Seeing the tenderness of my mom and the guidance of my dad, it sealed the deal for which fork in the road I wanted to follow.

Feeling motivated once again, I decided that I would do one more IUI with Dr. Rollins. I had it in me to do that much. It seemed a bit crazy to do a ninth IUI, but to be fair, only one of the previous eight had been with her. No one quits after one IUI. Especially one that sort-of worked.

CHAPTER 43

October, 2013

After spending time with my family, I dug down deep and found the energy I needed for one more push. At age 36, it felt premature to bow out completely. I started lining everything up for my next IUI, determined to make it my *last* IUI. I could not face another early miscarriage. I could not.

I asked the Reproductive Immunology clinic to perform their immune panel so that I could be cleared to cycle. I hadn't had any sort of testing since the IVF-miscarriage cycle the previous year, and I was praying that I didn't have to go to Mexico for LIT therapy again. When the nurse called with my results, she said that I did not have to do LIT - my numbers were super high! She said, "Whatever you are doing...keep doing it!" I wasn't sure what I was doing differently. Maybe it was Danica's magic, or being further along in healing my gut, or maybe it was fixing that stupid tooth!

Or all of those things! Either way, I was thrilled that I didn't have to squeeze in a last-minute trip to Mexico and even more thrilled that my body was more ready to receive a baby than it had ever been before.

We did the estrogen priming protocol, and when I started the fertility meds to make more eggs, we skipped Clomid in favor of the stronger injectable drugs. Dr. Peres, the RI, wanted me on a blood thinner, a steroid, and baby aspirin. Dr. Rollins, the RE, didn't see the need for the blood thinner. I was at a critical juncture here. *Who's advice do I follow?*

I thought about it long and hard. I refreshed my memory on the available research on blood thinners concerning fertility and immunology. I went back through my past cycles, reviewing what had worked and what hadn't. Under what circumstances had I miscarried? Why was it that the RI clinic wanted me on it again? When I boiled it all down, I came to the conclusion that I should be on it. Lovenox, in addition to being a blood thinner, also has an immunological effect. The dose I'd been prescribed was small, so it wasn't going to thin my blood enough to be dangerous. I wasn't going to bleed out if I cut myself or had an accident. I felt like it was only going to help and not hurt anything. I could be wrong of course, but it was time to pull out all the stops.

My body was responding really well to the fertility drug protocol Dr. Rollins designed. During my monitoring ultrasounds, I subtly covered up the purple dots on my tummy caused by the Lovenox injections. I wouldn't have lied about it if she noticed, but I didn't see the point of debating her either. I wished that we could have had more of a meeting of the minds and reached a protocol we all agreed on, but I had made up my mind. I would manage this on my own. And, I wouldn't put up with another miscarriage if there was something I could do to prevent it.

When we came in for the final ultrasound and IUI, Dr. Rollins saw eight mature follicles! That's more than I had ever had. It's also more than most doctors would feel comfortable utilizing with someone my age. But, knowing my history and odds of conception, Dr. Rollins felt that we were only risking three embryos implanting at best. Holding the syringe filled with my husband's processed semen up in the air like a loaded gun, she said, "Before I do this, you have to promise me that if three or more implant, you will consider a reduction."

We had to explain to Nile what "reduction" meant. A friend in my Resolve support group had shared that she, for medical reasons, had to reduce three babies to one. After battling infertility, being saddled with too many babies was almost unimaginable. Honestly, I couldn't imagine it. But, I heard her. I paused to thoroughly consider her request, and my intuition told me that it wouldn't come to that. So I agreed.

After the IUI, we drove down to Orange County to have lunch with Nile's mom who was visiting. We didn't tell her anything about the IUI; at this point, it was still our secret. During the two-week wait that followed, I was super busy at work. In fact, I was leading a vital project for my company that required round-the-clock attention and lots of oversight - so much for reducing my stress! Besides work, we watched a ton of college football and generally enjoyed ourselves.

About ten days after the IUI, I took a home pregnancy test. It was positive. I tried to be relaxed about it, but it was impossible not to feel a little excited. I repeated the test every day for the next four days. The first two were pretty faint, then the lines grew darker on the third and fourth tests. This was different than before, by the fourth day the line would usually start fading again. I emailed Dr. Rollins with the news and requested a blood test to confirm the pregnancy.

On Saturday morning, Dr. Rollins called with the results of our first beta. "Congratulations! You are pregnant!" she said. "Your numbers are really high for where you are in your pregnancy. Prepare yourself for multiples!" I stammered out a stunned response, "Uh...ok. I will!" She told me when to come back in for the follow-up betas. We said good-bye and I took a moment to absorb the news. It felt like I was floating. I couldn't believe it.

I remember exactly where I was standing in our condo when I received that phone call. The morning sun streamed through the floor-to-ceiling windows in our living room, warming up our home and hiding the chill of an early Fall. The dust and other particles in the air were caught in the stream of sunshine, adding a hazy glow, a natural filter that smoothed out all the edges of the hard times that had happened here. Time stood still, and I realized that something had fundamentally changed. All had not been lost. I'd restored myself, I'd found the right people to help me.

In that pause, I had a flashback to those dark days after the D&C, of standing with my husband in that exact same spot, telling him, "I don't want to be *me* anymore." My lowest low and my highest high had occurred in the same exact space.

My moment of calm was followed by a flash of panic! *What if I miscarry again? How will I survive it?* But my work with Danica permeated through those old patterns, and I reminded myself that, in this exact moment, I was fertile and very definitely pregnant.

We repeated the blood test two more times to track my numbers and make sure they were going up. I scrutinized my beta scores on a website called Betabase*. The numbers seemed to be in line with a twin pregnancy, but I couldn't be sure. We wouldn't know definitively until the ultrasound at seven weeks and two days gestation.

Even though my numbers looked great and I felt super pregnant, I was still nervous about the first ultrasound. The only time I had made it this far, I was dealt the devastating news that launched me into four months of pure hell. I wasn't sure I could survive that twice. It was incredible to be here again, but so scary.

The ultrasound was scheduled for the day before Thanksgiving. My parents were visiting again. This time, we didn't tell them about the IUI. I couldn't go down that road again - keeping everyone informed on the roller coaster ride that is repeated pregnancy loss. I hoped that the timing was a positive thing - that we would be able to stand together, surrounded by loved ones, when we made our announcement.

Nile came with me to the appointment for moral support and, hopefully, to see our baby (babies?) for the first time. When Dr. Rollins came into the room, she was bursting with happiness for us. I focused on soaking up all of her positive energy, trying to think only positive thoughts, but some part of me was still on guard. Getting quickly to the matter at hand, she began the ultrasound. Usually, I requested to watch the screen so I could see what was happening, but today I just couldn't. I couldn't bear the thought of looking at that screen and seeing those empty sacs again.

I lay there with my eyes closed, praying, listening, holding my husband's hand. The next few seconds would determine the final direction my life would take. This was the last fork in the road. *I will not miscarry again. It's these babies or no babies.*

After a few seconds, she said, "It looks like there are two!" My mind was waiting for the rest of it ("It looks like two tried to implant, but...") I asked her to repeat herself.

As I heard her announcement for the second time, everything released. The huge burden that I held inside flowed out of me. I cried and cried and cried. As soon as I composed myself, I asked her to show them to me. For the first time, I got to see my baby, my babies, there on the screen - two grainy black and white gummy bears dancing energetically in my womb.

This time was different. This time, I was a mom.

Epilogue

After the birth of our twins, I spent a lot of time talking to women who were still in the thick of their fertility struggle. Daily, I found myself forwarding resources and sharing my experiences with women who just needed to hear from someone who understood them. Eventually, I realized that my battle with infertility wasn't fading away in the rear view mirror of my new life like I had hoped. My story wasn't done with me yet.

So one day, during nap time, I started writing it down. As five years of test results and pain uncoiled onto paper, I didn't know why I was writing or who it was for - *Myself? My kids? Other couples still searching for answers?* I didn't know what I would do with it when it was done, but something inside of me kept pushing me to finish it.

In the midst of our infertility journey, I was focused on researching treatments and doctors, obsessing over test results and drug protocols. We were in the fog of war. Even in the whirlwind of raising twins, I was hounded by the feeling that I had *missed something*. I had a vague idea that writing down my story was beneficial to me, though I wasn't sure how or when the healing would be complete.

I often felt like it was frivolous of me to spend my time writing when I could be working a paying job or spending every minute with my kids. But I continued to write during stolen moments of my day. Every time I thought I'd finally captured all the essential details, new memories surfaced that I needed to process. Bit by bit, the pieces came together. I'd finished writing down almost every detail of my journey to conceive the twins, yet my work still felt unfinished.

Just as I reached this point, something unexpected happened - we conceived again. I'd recently turned 40, and with my history of infertility and autoimmune issues, it's a bit embarrassing to admit that this outcome had never occurred to me. I hadn't experienced a whiff of pregnancy in the three years since our twins were born. I sort of thought they were my last two good eggs. My cycles had grown erratic, and I experienced pain and anxiety at ovulation. I wasn't sure what was going on with my hormones and reproductive system, but I certainly did not feel like I was optimally fertile.

Now in my newly pregnant reality, I noticed the familiar pressing sensation in my uterus and pain in my breasts. My belly immediately expanded, my pants were tight even before the date of my missed period. On the outside, I carried on as usual, but my mind was spinning with the secret I kept. I wondered if perhaps my body had somehow been reset from those turbulent infertility days. Maybe all I needed to conceive spontaneously was to relax and not try at all; just like many well-meaning people had said. Lord knows having baby number three was the furthest thing from my mind.

I was not at all prepared to be a mom of three. Our house was too small. I'd given away all our baby gear as the kids outgrew it, convinced and completely satisfied that these would be our only children. Nile and I were both self-employed with unstable incomes and health insurance. What were we getting into? How could we have been so careless? Do I need to be on my old drug protocol to avoid a miscarriage? Was I putting my life at risk by getting pregnant again? My children need their mama.

On the fourth day of feeling early pregnancy symptoms, I ran into the dollar store to get a pregnancy test on the way home from a parent-and-me preschool class. I pulled three kits off the peg. As I handed them to the cashier, she looked at me and said, "Congratulaaaaaaaaations!" I bowed my head with embarrassment and gave her a quick grimace-smile as I swiped my debit card.

As soon as I could get my kids down for their nap, I took the pregnancy test, being careful to hide the packaging from Nile. I needed some time to process this before looping him in. I couldn't even guess what his reaction would be. But the test was negative. Hmmm. I decided to take another one in a couple of days. How sensitive were the dollar store tests again? Should I splurge on the high accuracy tests? I'd forgotten everything. However, none of that mattered because I never had the chance to test again.

The next day my pregnancy symptoms started fading; and like so many times before, I knew it was over. I found myself right where I had started eight years earlier, my infertility journey bookended with chemical pregnancies. When my period came, I felt like the lifeblood had been drained right out of me; for a couple of days, I barely had enough energy to function.

In the past, I was pretty quick to brush off early miscarriage effects like it was no big deal. I was a pull-yourself-up-by-your-bootstraps kind of girl, and I coped with my losses by working toward a solution. But now, I wasn't trying to find answers anymore. I was sitting with myself, fully experiencing this early loss without somewhere else to be.

Recalling all the prior miscarriages, I felt so much empathy for my old self: that young woman who kept facing these miscarriages over and over with no explanation and little help. If I could go back in time, I would tell her that these miscarriages are real and legitimate and that she, with full confidence, should bang on all the doors necessary to find the answers. *You are not making this up, and it is not normal. This is not God punishing you, it is not bad luck. These recurrent miscarriages are trying to tell you something.*

As my body bounced back from the miscarriage, I could finally see what the writing process was trying to teach me. It had been a three-year ordeal of revisiting and processing my infertility journey without knowing why I was doing it. But now, I understood.

By systematically scrutinizing the events of my infertility journey, I was able to make sense of it all. The clutter and the chatter were silenced. Instead of experiencing it in random flashbacks that my brain struggled to process out of context, or forgetting things entirely, the pieces were now organized and stored away in their proper order, like note cards in a drawer of my memory. It was a *story*, not just anecdotes swirling around in my head.

I felt settled, like I'd just cleaned out and organized the world's biggest closet.

Although I never completely stopped searching for a remedy for my infertility, I am crystal clear that there was no magic bullet. With my story organized, I could see exactly what was needed to resolve my infertility. *I needed all of it.*

I needed Reproductive Immunology and Western Medicine to calm my immune system and thin my blood so that our embryos were protected. I needed a fertility doctor that operated like a detective, dialing up a protocol just for me. I needed acupuncture and the woo-woo stuff to heal my mind and body and help me believe in myself again after so much loss. I needed a naturopath to help me change my diet to one that could heal me from the inside out. I needed to learn to listen to my body and let my intuition guide me. I needed the best doctors in Los Angeles to monitor my high-risk pregnancy and safely deliver our babies. I needed enough time to work all this stuff out.

And, I needed me. My perseverance, my stubborn hope in the possibility of success, failure after failure.

I was certain that if it weren't for my repeated efforts to find an explanation for my unexplained infertility and pregnancy loss, we would not have children. It wasn't a matter of relaxing and not trying, or drinking more green juice or doing more yoga or having more sex. It was a matter of healing my body and mind the best I could and blending intuition with science. It was finding the perfect combination that would allow my body to produce, accept, and protect our embryos so they could grow into healthy babies.

Without my infertility experience, I likely never would've known about the underlying autoimmunity in my body and never made the connection to the lifestyle I required, and still require, in order to heal. My story isn't over, and I'm not fully healed. I am a work in progress, and I'm still adding files to my baby binder.

ACKNOWLEDGMENTS

E ven with the clarity of how I got from Point A to Point Z, I am in awe of the miracle that is our happy ending. A million different things could have gone wrong, but in the end, they all went right one time.

I am in awe that my children are perfectly healthy and thriving. I am in awe that so many helpers showed up for me and still continue to do so. I couldn't have overcome infertility by myself, and I am forever grateful to those who showed me the way, gave me their knowledge and held my hand.

I remain indebted to the bountiful health and wellness community in Los Angeles, truly my City of Angels. I had everything I needed, exactly when I needed it, and that is nothing short of magical.

Specifically, I wish to thank Danica Thornberry and Dr. Kelly Baek for being part of the dream team that got me to the finish line. I also thank Resolve.org for the support they provided to me and continue to provide to other women struggling with infertility. Much appreciation to my editor Emma Fulenwider and all of the people who helped my story make the leap from my laptop to publication.

And to my husband, Nile, who holds my hand through all of it.

Discussion Questions:

How can you change your approach to infertility so that it is driven by curiosity instead of fear?

Are there areas of your health that you ignore or fail to maintain because you feel that they are "unrelated" to fertility?

How has your fertility struggle effected your relationships with friends and family?

What can you do to feel less isolated?

What do you do for fun?

What battles are you waging in your life?

Have you ever had to choose between trusting your doctor and listening to your intuition? (How can you work with your doctor to satisfy your intuition?)

Imagine that hope is a form of energy, how can you find it even in the darkest moments and use it to propel you forward?

RESOURCES:

Skin Deep Cosmetic Database: https://www.ewg.org/skindeep/

Taking charge of your Fertility: the definitive guide to natural birth control, pregnancy achievement and reproductive health, by Toni Weschler; Harper Collins, 1995

Making Babies: a proven 3-month program for maximum fertility, by Sami S. David and Jill Blakeway; Little, Brown and Company, 2009

"Reduction of blood flow impedance in the uterine arteries of infertile women with electro-acupuncture" by Elisabet Stener-Victorin, Urban Waldenstrom, Sven A. Andersson, Matts Wikland; Human Reproduction, Volume 11, Issue 6, 1 June 1996, Pages 1314–1317

MTHFR (methylenetetrahydrofolate reductase) "A Genetic Mutation That Can Affect Mental & Physical Health: MTHFR mutations are linked to depression, ADHD, migraines, miscarriage & more." by Traci Stein; PsychologyToday.com, Sep 05, 2014

The Paleo Mom, Dr. Sarah Ballantyne: https://www.thep-aleomom.com/

Is your Body Baby Friendly?: Unexplained Infertility, Miscarriage & IVF Failure - Explained and Treated, by Dr. Alan E. Beer; AJR Publishing, 2006

The Tao of Fertility: a healing Chinese medicine program to pre-pare body, mind and spirit for new life, by Daoshing Ni and Dana Herko; Harper Collins, 2008

BetaBase: http://www.betabase.info/

CPSIA information can be obtained
at www.ICGtesting.com
Printed in the USA
FSHW010448150119
55015FS

9 781545 652442